VANCOUVER
A City Album

VANCOUVER
A City Album

EDITORS
Anne Kloppenborg
Alice Niwinski
Eve Johnson
Introduction by David Brock

Douglas & McIntyre
Vancouver/Toronto

91 92 93 94 95   5 4 3 2 1

Third revised edition

Douglas & McIntyre
1615 Venables Street, Vancouver, British Columbia V5L 2Hl

Canadian Cataloguing in Publication Data
Main entry under title:
Vancouver, a city album
First-2nd eds. published as: Vancouver's first century.
ISBN 0-88894-705-4
1.Vancouver (B.C.)—History. I. Kloppenborg, Anne.
II. Niwinski, Alice. III. Johnson, Eve. IV. Title: Vancouver's first century.
FC3847.37.V35 1991 971.1'33   C91-091009-X
F1089.5.V22V35 1991

Design by Simon Bishop
Design consultant: Nancy Grout

Printed and bound in Canada by D. W. Friesen & Sons Ltd.

Contents

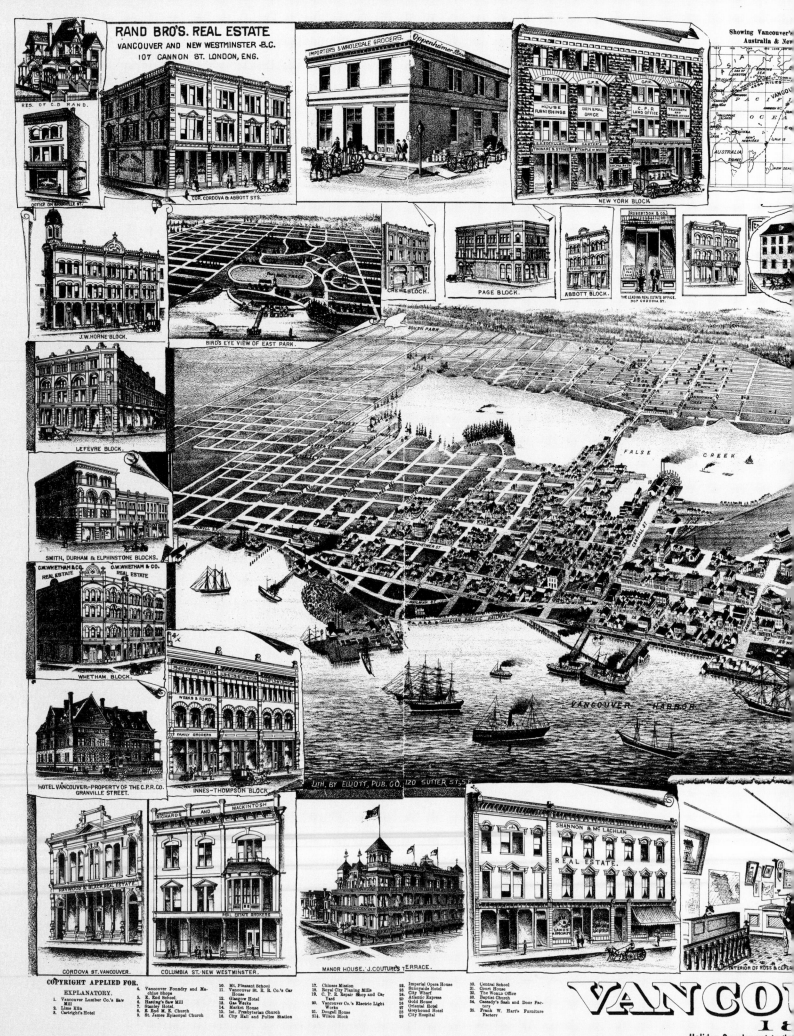

Preface

Since Vancouver is now well past its first hundred years, this volume, the third edition of what was originally called *Vancouver's First Century*, has been renamed *Vancouver: A City Album* and expanded to cover the years 1860 to 1990. Our project started life in 1975 as a series of special historical issues of the magazine *Urban Reader*. The book was first published in 1977 and revised in 1985 to cover the period up to Vancouver's Centennial. This updated edition reveals a city entering a period of dramatic change after Expo 86, documenting Vancouver's rich and growing ethnic diversity, as well as the first phase of massive redevelopments on the north shore of False Creek and at Coal Harbour.

Capturing Vancouver's most recent past proved to be a very different challenge from documenting the city's beginnings. In both the second and third editions, we had thousands of photos to choose from and more written records than we could possibly use. The problem was immediacy: the last decades are a little close for historical perspective. We hope our interpretation rings true for our readers, present and future.

News photos and stories from the city's two leading dailies form the backbone of both the second and third editions. Special thanks are due to *Vancouver Sun* and *Vancouver Province* editors Shelley Fralic and Ian Haysom for their generosity in allowing us access to the Pacific Press photographic collection. The pamphlet files of the Vancouver City Archives and the collections of the Vancouver Public Library Historical Photographs Division were a rich resource. Thanks are also due Anna Sumpter of the Vancouver City Archives, Leslie Ross and many other helpful staff members of the Vancouver Public Library, as well as Hayne Wai who shared his Strathcona photographs with us.

We are also grateful to photographers Henri Robideau, Fred Herzog, David Jacklin and Bev Davies for the striking images they contributed.

On the research side, our thanks go back to Robert Gruetter who contributed to the first edition and to Sue Fisher and Helen Hossie who assisted with the second edition. Nancy Knickerbocker, a Vancouver free-lance writer who grew up here, contributed her knowledge and perceptiveness to the research of images and excerpts for the third edition.

We thank the Director of Social Planning, Joyce Preston, and the Senior Cultural Planner, Burke Taylor, for encouraging and supporting our work on this edition. Research and materials for both the second and third editions were paid for through the city's Publishing Reserve Trust Account. Royalties go back to the city to support the City of Vancouver Book Award and other projects to assist Vancouver writers. Our thanks to Vancouver City Council for their continuing support.

Preface to the First Edition

In some ways this book has been more than 100 years in the making. It owes its existence to pioneer photographers who captured telling images with the most primitive equipment, early journalists, families who saved diaries and photo albums, archivists who sought out the scraps of history in attics.

The early photographers — men such as H.T. Devine, Philip Timms, C.S. Bailey, William Notman and Stuart Thomson — needed skill, intuition and patience to record the city's development. They changed the focus of their heavy wooden cameras by adjusting leather bellows, they used removable metal plates with different sized holes to control the aperture, and they regulated exposure time by taking off the lens cap, counting, and replacing it. Exposure times were so long that if anything in the picture moved, it showed up either as a blur or not at all.

As we sifted through the material which has found its way into the Vancouver City Archives, the Provincial Archives, and the Vancouver Public Library's Historical Photograph Section and Northwest Reading Room, we came to appreciate how precarious the survival of history is. The fire of 1886 consumed many records, but even in better times, thousands of fragile glass plates and nitrate negatives have been lost. Someone used George T. Wadd's entire collection of glass negatives to build a greenhouse — after washing off the emulsion. Other photographers' plates have been found in chicken coops and basements, the negatives damaged by rain and rat droppings. Even under ideal conditions, nitrate negatives will eventually destabilize, heat up and burst into flame. To avoid such spontaneous combustion the Vancouver Fire Marshall's office rounded up all the nitrate film it could find in 1954, and destroyed it. Most of the work had never been copied, and was lost.

Like many cities, Vancouver left the preservation of its earlier years to eccentric collectors, compulsive letter writers and other amateurs. Many of the City's written records — not to mention informative trivia such as dance programs and war posters — would not have survived except for the determination of Major J.S. Matthews, who appointed himself Vancouver's first archivist long before the City grudgingly recognized his work.

While chance and the biases of collectors like Matthews have, in effect, pre-selected the material available to us, the process of finding photographs, anecdotes and other items reflecting ten decades of the city's growth has been a long one. It would have been impossible without the expertise and work of many people in the community. For their help we thank the City Archivist, Sue Baptie, and her staff, as well as the previous archivist, Lynn Ogden; Vancouver Public Library's Historical Photograph Section curator Ron D'Altroy and his staff; New Westminster Public Library head Alan Woodland; the Provincial Archives; the Notman Photographic Archives at McGill University. We are grateful to photographers Jack Lindsay, Bill Cunningham and Fred Herzog, still working in the city, who came forward with pictures of the '40s and '50s not available in any archives. We would also like to thank Professor Norbert Macdonald of the UBC History Department, Jacquie Stevens of the Historical Photograph Section and Dave Brock for their advice, and all the other people who provided a useful picture, detail or opinion.

The production of this book would have been impossible without the continuing support of Ernie Fladell from the City of Vancouver's Social Planning Department, who three years ago suggested an *Urban Reader* magazine on Vancouver's history, or the endorsement of the Social Planning Director, Maurice Egan. Ernie's idea turned into a special issue, "Vancouver: Turn of the Century," which was so popular that we followed it with four additional historical magazines over the next two years. The five issues, greatly expanded and edited, are the basis of this book.

We were fortunate to have the services of excellent local photographers in developing prints of the old photographs we have used. It takes a patient and skilled hand to turn a damaged glass negative into a clear print, and we thank Henry Robideau, Emily Grice and Fred Douglas for their careful work.

We also thank the people who are not now on the *Urban Reader* staff but who worked on the first historical issues: Gary Wilcox, Margaret Fahlman and George Payerle.

In reprinting excerpts from diaries, newspapers and memoirs, we have left the stylistic quirks intact. The "drunket and disorderly persons" and the "type-writers [and] shopgirls" remain as we found them.

The Editors

Introduction

There is a camera which, if set up at Ferguson Point in cool and steady air, can not only photograph an eagle's nest in Lighthouse Park, six miles away, but also zoom in to give details of the twigs and eaglets. Much the same effect is managed within these covers by means of detailed close-ups that cross the years instead of the miles. The album's selection provides for an agreeable blend of learning and lively enjoyment; of essential-to-know major facts and delightfully trivial-seeming discoveries that really do bring our past to life. The mixture of formal structure with random sampling achieves a pleasant kind of unity. Time and time again the editors bring immediacy to some tiny old forgotten far-off thing.

I am pleased and touched to be asked to write the introduction to this very enterprising Vancouver family album, for I am not quite what used to be called proudly, and even snobbishly, a Native Son. I was born in Ottawa and did not live in Vancouver until I was four, but at the top of every list of 101 remarkable things about our city is the fact that new arrivals from anywhere are converted into Vancouverites by some benign influence as swift as it is magical. And since my conversion has stood the test of over 60 years, perhaps I am now eligible, at that, to wish the book long life and good health.

I have spent about twenty-five years in the nostalgia trade. (Nostalgia is the wrong word, mind you, for it is really a medical term which means a homesickness that incapacitates the patient. A soldier with genuine nostalgia is sent home on sick leave, for he has become useless and dangerous. Dogs can die of it, and do.) I grow wistful about the delights of a world now vanished: foods and drinks and books and magazines; theatres and actors and musicians; styles and characters and vanished opinions; a couple of dozen writers; modes of travel of a comfort now unimaginable; hotels and once-lovely places at the end of a restful journey; decent tobacco; a less noisy world; beer without additives (a thing that no longer exists anywhere!); statesmen, Pantagruelism — "a certain jollity of mind pickled in the scorn of fortune"; real flannel, real silk, real leather, real wood; a capacity to amuse oneself in a world where everyone was his own circus and where very few games had yet been turned into work — and where, I must add, work had not been turned into a farcical sort of frittering. While reading last night about the CPR's Princess ships that once made this coast so lively and pleasant, I was astonished to find that not only did the *Princess Patricia II* and the *Princess Marguerite II* of the late 1940s cost three or four times as much as the very comparable *Princess Kathleen* and the *Princess Marguerite I* of the middle 1920s but also they took about three times as long to build.

Which brings me to the subject of vanished prices. Yes, I get wistful about those, too, as who does not? When my brothers and I were housekeeping in the depression years of 1935-37, we treated ourselves to one joint of meat a week. In those days, David Spencer Limited had a food market on the southwest corner of Fourth and Vine, and on Saturdays I would journey there to pick up a shoulder of lamb at nine cents a pound as our extravagance for Sunday. I wish an archivist would publish a catalogue showing how prices have changed over the years. Old newspaper files tell you (naturally) only about items that were advertised. I have figures for the reign of King Henry VIII, when the poor complained about having to live on eggs and chicken and beef and cheese and beer and dark bread, because they could not afford the white wheaten bread of the gentry! I also know that in the reign of his daughter Elizabeth, a caged seagull fed on beef liver or grain or curds from the dairy to improve its flavour would be sold for five shillings (to the Lords of the Star Chamber anyhow), and also get praised for being absolutely delicious. For that same five shillings (a huge sum in those days) you could have bought 42 pounds of beef.

This is not absolutely to the point, in a book about our city, but even in my lifetime, luxuries and economical fare can trade places drastically. Only a few decades ago, poor people in British Columbia (and in England too) did not greatly care for having to dine too often on a tin of salmon. Today canned salmon is almost a treat, and usually merits fancy treatment. Again, in my youth, calves' sweetbreads were given away free to the butcher's better customers, and I imagine he gave away kidneys as well. Today you pay dearly for sweetbreads, and I feel wistful, but not so nostalgic that I want the doctor to make a house call.

There must be hundreds of things I feel slightly regretful and pensive about, now that they are gone. A few will return. Roses with a rich scent are back again, saved in the nick of time in the 1960s, and are now quite a fad. How we would have laughed at that in 1920, on our five-block walk to Kitsilano School on any fine June morning, when smelling a few dozen roses along the way was a good method of retaining a jollity of mind pickled in the scorn of education. My brother Tommy got so good at taking his mind off his troubles by smelling flowers and foliage that once, while sniffing a pussywillow branch too vigorously, he inhaled one of the furry catkins and required surgical intervention to be rid of it. We thought at first that it had entered his brain. Anything can happen in spring, when all nature is on the move.

My approach to the past usually tends to be more curious than mournful, and I feel that it is fairly important to greet the past as an equal rather than feeling either superior or inferior to it. Naturally, I laugh at it quite often, but only as I laugh at much of the present and at what little I know about the future. Some of the objects of my curiosity about the past, and my ways of satisfying and enjoying this curiosity, may appear trivial or irresponsible or disrespectful to some readers. I indeed blow up trifles by means of extreme close-ups with my six-mile lens, but in blowing up trifles, initially for enjoyment, one often discovers that such a close scrutiny can have its use too. G.K. Chesterton, who was a great man for poking around in other people's accepted ideas, implied all this in a two-word title, "Tremendous Trifles."

Two or three examples will suffice. Gassy Jack is a trivial subject that is doubly important, because in laughing at the important place accorded him in Vancouver, I am not mocking the past at all but rather the present. We try to make an interesting hero of him today, yet he was a bore. His contemporaries laughed at him for being a bore, hence his nickname. Obviously he had a neurotic or psychotic symptom known as logomania, sometimes called logorrhea, which is loquacity too loose and frequent and often accompanied by griping pains — for others rather than for the patient. In what other part of the world has a statue ever been erected to such a tedious old pest? For a town with almost no statues, it is amazing that we have raised monuments to two such tiresome creatures, the other being the embarrassing and hilarious tribute to President Harding in Stanley Park.

Far from my being discourteous to the past (and to the disciples of Major Matthews who hold that everyone before 1900 was fascinating and noble), I have for 50 years gone out of my way to pronounce Gassy Jack's surname correctly, which is more than his promoters do. The only Deighton I ever met assured me that all Deightons worthy of the name do not rhyme is with Satan; no, they rhyme it with Brighton.

There are less controversial trifles that are even more trivial. Ever since the streetcars stopped running, a long and merry time ago, I have revived old streetcar memories, rerunning them like home movies. On the sound track there is a good assortment of special effects such as the motorman's warning gong, which he clanged by treading on a kind of iron mushroom whose stem went down through the floor of his cab. When the brakes went on hard, the wheels sounded like the results of many costly but ineffectual violin lessons. The malevolent squealing was not unlike that of some huge, cornered rat. You will note that we rustic poets compare the sound with fiddles and wildlife. But I have heard a city boy object to an irksome little violinist's efforts by saying that he sounded like a streetcar stopping. In *The Napoleon of Notting Hill*, long out of print, Chesterton draws our attention to the fundamental opposition of these two kinds of poet. The country poet will say that his cab is swift as the wind, but a true city poet will say that the wind swings around the corner as sudden and swift as a cab. That is still another tremendous trifle. I can tell from the kinds of poetry I write that I do not automatically love all city life but love only Vancouver.

We never called the urban streetcars "trams." Trams were the larger and faster interurban cars that ran through Burnaby to New Westminster, or up the south side of the Fraser to Chilliwack, or across Lulu Island to Steveston. "Trolleycar" was another expression used only by visitors.

There was a conductor on the Fourth Avenue line who liked to pass the time, as we whirled through Kitsilano, by trying to give two pronunciations to as many street names as possible, so that as two men got off at Balaclava, one would be under the impression that he was atBala-CLA-va, while the other was sure that he had heard "Balacla-VAH." And thus with DUN-bar and (more correctly) Dun-BAR. With Tra-FAL-gar and TRA-falgar this simple street-singer on wheels had quite by accident hit upon a crux that has embittered naval historians (and Spaniards) for over 170 years.

But of all the streetcar sounds, by far the best remembered is the noise that came from under our feet each time the car paused. The noise said "Lugga-lugga-lugga-lugga-lug" and when my brothers and I were small, we found this voice and its magic word to be interesting, authorative, reassuring, and much else. It meant that all was well, and it also imparted some of the romance of travel. As for what it meant and where it came from, it never occurred to us to wonder. It may, I now realize, have had something to do with the air-brake system, if streetcars have air brakes.

And here is one trifle so small that its very dimensions make me smile. John Barrymore's large and famous schooner was anchored off Jericho Beach, to grace some international regatta of the 1920s. During the Prohibition period, the Pacific International Yachting Association held two thirds of its regattas in Canada (mostly in Vancouver) for at least one obvious reason best summed up in a now forgotten but once hackneyed folk song:

Four and twenty Yankees, feeling very dry
Sailed across to Canada to get a case of rye.
When the case was opened, they all began to sing
"To hell with the President and God save the King."

The chief problem of Prohibition was one of quality rather than quantity, and the great John Barrymore, in his crises of lucidity, was ever eager to delay the final stages of that other folk song "The Wreck of the John B." So there he lay at anchor off Jolly Jerry Rogers' Cove, about three cables from my house. As I rowed round and round the schooner one evening, sounds of revelry poured from every open scuttle. My rowing and musings were interrupted by an empty bottle that hurtled out of one of those open scuttles and nearly brained me. I took that bottle reverently ashore and built a little shrine for it in the wildest part of our garden where common fingers and eyes could never profane it.

I no longer think that movie stars are divine in any sense whatever, and here the majority and I agree comfortably. The realization that "these harlotry players" are all too human, if not sub-human, is one of the surest proofs that while many parts of civilization grow sillier, others eventually mature. But to this day I still think that the Barrymore schooner herself was somewhat divine.

Oh my, oh my, the yachts of our youth! I was always vaguely sorry that Vancouver had nothing larger than 200 feet, but B. T. Rogers's steam yacht *Aquilo*, which came round Cape Horn in 1912, was 168 feet, and by coincidence the *Moolight Maid* (ex *Lady Stimson* ex *Stadacona* ex *Columbia*) was also 168 feet. The latter, having been an RCN vessel and a deep-sea rum runner (among other things) ended up as a Seattle-Alaska tug in World War II. She must have made a very long tug: "a long pull and a strong pull and a pull all together." And when she was filled with rum, she could have sung the same song to a different meaning.

We knew at the time that the big yachts were impressive, even when not too shapely, but we had no idea that they would disappear, priced out of the market. Half a century ago and more, Mrs. J.P. Morgan, Jr., told my New York aunt that the costs of the 300-odd-foot *Corsair* were ridiculous, consuming $300,000 a year just to be kept tied up and idle. Today I suppose that the sum would be several millions.

Later we would be impressed by the very high quality of Vancouver-built rowboats, small open motorboats, and tiny dinghies. Also, we took for granted the quality of Lakefield and Peterborough canoes shipped out from Ontario. By 1930, incidentally, I seemed to be the only person on local waters who appreciated the joy and exhilaration of sailing a canoe, and I bought that year the last canoe sail and pair of leeboards to be found here. Among thousands of mysterious disappearances, this is one of the oddest.

Threefold mourning must be given the design and materials and workmanship of the clinker-built open boats by Turner or Linton. One can perhaps be philosophical about a mere shortage of decent woods, but not about their vanishing. Eastern boatyards come to Vancouver Island looking for good oak while westerners go east on the same vain quest. Not even good spruce is likely any more, on this of all coasts. Do you remember the hand-made spoon-bladed good spruce oars at maybe $5 a pair? Try to get some now at any price. Ask your friendly local hardware man for a nice hickory axe handle or shovel handle, and stand clear before he troubles deaf heaven with his bootless cries.

The years I "wasted" on Vancouver waters were not merely therapeutic. If you wait long enough the sea will bring you anything, including alder logs for your fireplace, kelp to improve your soil, salt air to improve your asparagus and sea holly and rosemary (among other plants), and highly dramatic rainsqualls and fog — thus furnishing, for the fanciful, the four "elements" of earth, air, fire and water. But these are only the beginning. It has brought to me lumber, furniture, a new down pillow (off the late lamented Night Boat to Victoria), several small boats, two dead seals for the rose garden, pike poles, buoys, nylon rope. The list could go on. Not only does it include food taken directly, such as salmon, grilse, ling cod, skate, flounders, tommy cod, rock cod, red snappers, smelts, herring and crabs (does the Big Hole off Jericho still fill up with crabs, or have the currents filled up the hole itself?) but also in our Kitsilano days we got food indirectly by gathering ready-crushed mussel shells from Trafalgar Beach to feed our hens for their calcium intake, to toughen their eggshells. The backyard hens of Kitsilano are probably no more.

One of Vancouver's most stirring events is the strange blue and white daylight that so often visits during bright springs and autumns. You notice and enjoy it much more by sea than by land. On the other hand, the far rarer and stranger violet light that comes here only in the luckiest of early Aprils, along the North Shore mountains, can be seen from the First Narrows bridge quite as well as from a boat, and perhaps better. Only one traveller that I know of has mentioned it in print, and until he came here he had thought it peculiar to Ireland. No Vancouver writer has mentioned it. Not that the best things are improved by chatter: some of them are ruined, or go away. W.B. Yeats said it is wrong to speak of ghosts overmuch, for you attract the rascals, and I know at first hand that this is true.

But in the home movies of my memory, one of the most romantic debts to the sea has been the wildlife, much of it no longer to be seen here. Killer whales (at that time called blackfish) used to swim east through English Bay and into the inner harbour through the First Narrows before every major storm, and this they did in large numbers, as many as thirty or forty of them. The last time I saw them was about thirty years ago, and by then it was a rare sight. The last time I saw porpoises playing alarmingly near my tiny Turner dinghy, off 29th Street in West Vancouver, was about 1940. Also about then a deer wandered down to the beach (near 31st Street in West Vancouver) and another was seen swimming westward parallel to the beach. One day a bear poked his head through our gate on Procter Avenue, but backed out again. Two peregrine falcons landed on a great flat boulder on our beach, and once two very powerful black gyrfalcons flew in from the west with the utmost speed and grace and purpose, and then turned north up Hollyburn Ridge, although the books say that they shun civilization. The books claim that ravens also avoid the haunts of men, which is absurd. The streets of Prince Rupert are full of them, or used to be. Our local ones used to haunt Lighthouse Park, until camps filled with Junior Forest Wardens in red shirts made the ravens fly away, not from the big city but towards it. Several settled on our beach, where they fought the local cats for the right to kill the toothed but non-venomous water snakes known as wandering garter snakes. The ravens always won, against both cats and snakes. Today the snakes and the ravens have died off or gone elsewhere. Eagles have been increasing in recent years, I am glad to say, and are becoming far more eccentric in their behaviour. Several go close past my windows every day, some of them lingeringly.

Land otters used to breed under Burrard Bridge, of all places, and were filmed around 1960, but I doubt if they come back any more. Twenty-odd years ago a sea otter raised her two pups a few yards from my house. They lived on the beach and just offshore for maybe three glorious months. It was a daily joy even to see her wondrous fur as she lay on her back in the water and thoughtfully lowered fish into her mouth with her hands.

I should think that the mother sea otter was what the *Reader's Digest* would call The Most Unforgettable Character I Ever Met. There were human ones, too, of course, many of them strangers. When Vancouver was smaller, and downtown was really the centre of just about everything, you never went there without meeting friends on every block, and several familiar strangers as well. There was a little man, oddly dressed, with an affliction that made him walk like Charlie Chaplin, so that everyone for decades *called* him Charlie. And since he kept pretty well to the northern end and western side of Granville Street, he was often to be seen (walking frontwards, backwards or sideways, and even with one foot on the curb and the other in the gutter) outside the old White Lunch at Pender and Granville where the *real* Charlie Chaplin is said to have washed dishes for a few days while waiting for his U.S. visa.

I don't think that Charlie really attempted to look like Chaplin, but there was a man who certainly tried to look like George V, complete with identical moustache and beard to make sure no one thought the astonishing effect accidental. This duplicate of our reigning monarch made loyalists fume, while the tiny republican element enjoyed its daily snicker.

Being a Character can pay off. The amazingly unkempt and noisy eccentric "Professor Francis," on the strength of having printed some musical criticisms, was by Vancouver custom admitted free not only to concerts and recitals but also to plays, movies and (if anyone tipped him off) private musical evenings in people's houses. God help any new doorman who didn't know these unlikely rules. The Professor would yell at him loud and long.

It was impossible to recognize Boris Karloff on Granville Street, because he did not assume that name and character until he left us for Hollywood, but under his true name of Bill Pratt he doubled as a longshoreman on the Vancouver waterfront and a stage hand at the older of the two Orpheums. Before that he had acted in a stock company at Kamloops, where "stock" normally means "cattle."

To me, as to thousands of others, a most memorable downtown eccentric to be seen and heard daily was Whistling Texas. He carried a sandwich board to urge us to try the Union Steamships cruises, and as he shuffled along he whistled a vast repertoire of tunes with the utmost energy and skill. He never stopped and he never tired. He was said to have damaged his head by getting it caught between a steamer and a wharf. If that was the cause of his enormous happiness, then more people should try it. We were more easily pleased in those days than we are now, no criticism of our own brains implied. One of my favourite sayings is that gaiety is the courage of the intelligent. There is another saying, which old Anatole France never wearied of repeating, that men are better than nature. Nobody could be more grateful than I am for Vancouver's very special contacts with nature, so plentiful in my youth, and a fair selection of them persisting even now. But Whistling Texas outdid even the western meadowlarks (before they moved out of town). He was the cheerfullest sound of Vancouver.

I suppose that the most astonishing sound of Vancouver came one night in the summer of 1936 when the roof of the Denman Street Arena fell in as the huge old place burned down. At 16th and Granville, two and a half miles from Coal Harbour, it was considered a really splendid noise. In any list of the world's best titles we should include Frank Sullivan's "The Night the Old Nostalgia Burnt Down." The old arena had nostalgia aplenty. For a long time it had the world's biggest rink, and it seated 10,000. On that ice played the world's first professional hockey league — Vancouver, Victoria and Seattle, all owned by the Patrick brothers, with the Vancouver club bearing the unlikely name of

"Millionaires." Each of the three teams won the Stanley Cup once, in their early NHL days, or in playoffs against the NHL.

On public skating days the arena had a live band. It was a time when everybody had a band. Even the Vancouver Parks Board had a band. Under Lieutenant Cornfield the Parks Board Band graced at least three bandstands that I recall: in Stanley Park, and the little English Bay triangle called Alexandra Park (where the Easter sunrise service was often held), and in a bandstand east of the Kitsilano bathing beach, at the eastern end of the boardwalk. I know one Vancouver private garden that still has a boardwalk, but no bandstand.

I think that Galli-Curci sang in the Arena, with no help from any public address system, and I know that other singers did. I don't mean the little Denman Auditorium outside the Arena, I mean the big hockey palace itself. But the finest vocal *tour de force* ever heard in either of those buildings was the night a heckler asked Mackenzie King "Where were you in the Great War?" and Billy King drew himself up proudly and cried out, "I was at the Post of Duty!" Those seven tiny words contained tunes of glory, and recruiting speeches galore, and all of them bewitching. It brought the house down, enraptured. (Actually, Billy King's post had been in Colorado or somewhere, writing a labour report for the Rockefellers.)

Some of Vancouver's best cheering was held in constant readiness for the zoo's large bear named Trotsky; I think he came from Siberia, but he was certainly of the huge Alaskan type. We were told that he was the biggest bear in captivity and perhaps even in history, so we felt huge ourselves, for such is civic pride and ambition. For similar reasons we were ever ready with proud cheers for the immense age of a man known to us all as Dad Quick, as he reached 110, then 111, then 112. Unfortunately, when he died loaded with honours it was discovered that he was only eighty-odd. It was much the same when Trotsky died. Somebody foolishly weighed him, and he tipped the scale at 750 pounds or something very like that. This is rather different from the 1,800-pound Alaskan bear that holds the real record.

On the other hand, among Vancouver's many real records, the most astonishing one (to me anyhow) is almost completely forgotten and was never widely known. You will not find it in many books, if any. The world's tallest trees, accurately measured, are said to be the Californian coast redwoods, with the highest reaching just under 370 feet — although various eucalyptus trees have been reputed to grow to 375 feet, the biggest scientifically measured eucalyptus reached only 322 feet. A Douglas fir felled in 1940 at Lynn Valley, in the Vancouver area, was properly measured at 417 feet. Loggers tell me that in Victorian times some bigger ones were almost certainly felled, not only in the suburbs but right in what is now downtown. The big firs around Granville and Georgia were whoppers.

To insist on beating all records at all costs, and then boasting about it, is of course unseemly. Two of my favourite Vancouver memories concern complete modesty and indifference about records. One is of a UBC girl who in 1930 (or so) beat the world's high jump record for women while merely amusing herself, and in tennis shoes at that. She had witnesses, but she wasn't interested in using them. All she wanted was a cup of tea. She would have liked Calverley, the English poet, who beat the world's high jump record by about a foot on a ballroom floor in evening dress and dancing shoes. The other memory is of a woman at Jericho who caught a 95-pound salmon in the swirling waters off Point Atkinson. One of my brothers saw it, but the world did not. She had it all in tins that same afternoon, and not in the newspapers at all. I do not interpret such interesting silences, but I appreciate them, and in any comprehensive list of Vancouver sounds they should go in as anti-sounds.

One of the most exciting sounds was so faint and sweet, it could awaken only the nervous or sick. Normal sleepers were wakened by the many morning sawmill whistles. But if you happened to be already awake at three or four on a winter morning and heard sleigh bells, you knew that your horse-drawn milkman was using a sled instead of a wagon. Vancouver snow was almost as rare in the past as it is now. News photos of our 1916 snow went all over the world, and the 1935 fall collapsed the roof of the Forum, but those were twice-in-a-lifetime affairs.

During the Kaiser's War we were awakened many and many a night by newsboys running through the suburbs crying "Extra! Extra! War Extra!" Another wartime sound was rifle fire in the basement range of Kitsilano Public School. Elementary school took us through Grade VIII in those days, so many of the older cadets were 13 or even 14.

Our first traffic lights rang bells each time they changed, in case the drivers and pedestrians were blind or dozing. One night Prince Henry, Duke of Gloucester, uncle to our present Queen, was brought back to his Hotel Vancouver suite with his arm broken in a polo game. To ensure a restful night for HRH, the police silenced the bell on the traffic lights at Georgia and Granville. Far from producing silence, this action produced a public outcry about pampered Royalty endangering lives. I don't quite remember anyone comparing this wicked Duke with Jenghis Khan, who killed 1,600,000 civilians in a single day, but the implication was there, all right. Today we seem not to care about traffic lights being silent.

Each morning at 9:00 a giant handbell, brandished by the reigning teachers' pet (female), would summon us to fall in on the school playground and march indoors in a para-military manner while the other pet (male) hoisted the Union Jack. It did us no lasting harm whatever. Other handbells were heard at the Vancouver Exhibition in Hastings Park (now the PNE), where the best meals were served in tents operated by several rival churches. The clergy rang handbells outside and acted as barkers to lure us in for the manly soups and dainty dumplings and pies. These dishes, some lyrical and some epic, bring me to the tastes, the smells and tactile impressions of early Vancouver.

We used to dig warm soft tar out of the joints between the concrete sidewalk blocks, and this we would chew. In many families, chewing gum was absolutely forbidden, but parents rarely thought to forbid sidewalk tar. My brothers flavoured their tar with fresh mint, and since menthol is a ring-carbon they probably doubled their risk of cancer from the tar. Rising to nobler foods, there were cent-candies now unknown, including chocolate-coated teddy bears. In the infinitely more heavenly vacant lots we ate the peeled salmonberry shoots locally called muck-a-muck, though in the Chinook jargon this means simply food, or to bite and eat. Salmonberry shoots would be "salmon olillie tenas stick." We drank honey from bleeding-heart blossoms and wild honeysuckle and clover and nasturtiums, and we smoked either cubebs (an asthma cigarette now gone, and very peppery) or wild spiraea rolled in newspaper (rather poisonous) or smoked in clay pipes bought at the barber's for a nickel, a frequent cause of mouth cancer. The infinite supply of enormous hollow stumps made wonderful places to hide in. By more grown-up standards, the apples of those days were memorable, because they were picked fairly ripe and were grown in soil onto which irrigation had not yet dumped an overdose of alkali.

As for the sense of touch, I mentioned a fabric or two, but should have added real velvet. I have a velvet dinner jacket of the early 1930s and everyone wants to stroke me before I can take it off and put up my dukes. And there were ladies who arrived with glorious fur muffs. Crofter-made Harris tweed was as fragrant as it was soft and beautiful, from the smell of the peat, and in Vancouver's rainy weather it smelled better still.

I also pat, for luck and friendship, the Bute Street yew tree (outside the Banff) and the Blanca Street arbutus, both probably here long before the white kids and their loggers and fires came. The arbutus is six miles from its habitat, across the water, so it must have arrived inside a bird who ages ago sank into the deeps of time.

As for old Vancouver smells, high on my own list were the western red cedar shingle mills, and the boat yards using yellow cedar. Not that I scorn Douglas fir. They all made my home town more like home. So does alder smoke. So does the subtle scent of dogwood blossoms. In my part of town at least the dogwoods are multiplying rapidly, so we do improve in some ways, even if the architect Henry Elder calls ours the ugliest city on earth and Pierre Burton reckons that we have not a single asset except the southern tip of the Coast Range, which (he says) we imagine we built by hand. No, we did not make the mountain skyline, but a skyline always makes the inhabitants. The late A.J.T. "Fred" Taylor in the 1930s told me that Vancouver is a first-rate place filled with second-rate people. He was the man who conceived and developed the British Properties and built the First Narrows bridge and cut Stanley Park in half to reach the bridge. He also discovered the Lagoon fountain lying idle after the Chicago World Fair and got it here it time for Mayor McGeer's 1936 Jubilee, pronounced Jubbalee.

Myself, I do not wish to analyse Vancouver and its people at all by systematic reasoning and confident insolence. It is better to "love her still and know not why, so dote upon her ever," as the old anonymous madrigal says. But one is allowed to suspect that the hills and water are involved, and old Zephyrus, the warm west wind as yet unpolluted. When I went barefoot in Kitsilano (often pronounced "Kitsilana" to rhyme with "Dinah") we daily got splinters under our toenails from the planked road along York Street and the board sidewalk on Larch. This was a useful lesson, teaching us while young that life is full of splinters. Vancouver has had countless mistakes and misfortunes and will have plenty more, both naturally and unnaturally. But so far, its faults and losses have defied the laws of physics and justice by not subtracting much from its total good.

When we were a year or two into the Depression, somebody in Vancouver decreed a Prosperity Week to end the Depression as a mere state of mind. All it caused was a series of misadventures, ending with a really big one when the brand new Canadian National pier at the foot of Main Street burned down. The smoke from a big burning wharf is a heavy black, from all that creosote on the pilings. We all laughed, but not from a spirit of vandalism. No, it was the name and aim of Prosperity Week that did it, compared with the results. Such unexpected and useful hilarity used to mark the Cockneys, and certain Africans, and well it served them, too, until it was educated out of them quite lately. I hope that a little of it persists along Burrard Inlet. But if we keep analysing ourselves to the verge of lunacy, which is another effect of education, we shall lose our identity. "And all that the old Duke had been without knowing it, the young Duke would fain know he was without being it."

Here I must stop, for fear of being elected Gassy Jack the Second. Of the few small memories I mentioned at random, out of thousands unspoken, could not some have happened anywhere else? No doubt, but they could not have happened in a better place or left me nodding quite so benignly to my own past.

David Brock

Prologue

Sea-otter pelts sold well in China in the late 1700s: so well that as Britain pursued the trade along North America's western coastline, she nearly came to blows with Spain, which claimed the area as her own. When Captain George Vancouver sailed into the waters behind Vancouver Island in 1792 his two missions were to negotiate with Spanish officials at the Nootka Sound outpost and to map the shoreline which was Britain's last hope of finding the northwest passage.

Burrard Inlet, which he discovered and mapped in June of that year, was no answer to Britain's quest. Had Vancouver been able to talk to the Indians from Whoi-Whoi (at Lumberman's Arch in Stanley Park) and Whumulcheson (at the mouth of the Capilano), who met his ships with gifts of smelt, he might also have found the Fraser River. Instead, he met a Spanish party under Dionisio Alcalá Galiano and Cayento Valdez and, to his chagrin, learned that José Maria Narváez had discovered the river the previous year. It was a blot on Vancouver's otherwise careful work.

He continued north towards Nootka, mapping as he went. Then, for over half a century, while Spain's influence waned and Britain cemented its claim to island and mainland by establishing Victoria and Fort Langley, the wilderness which would become Vancouver lay undisturbed.

In 1858, the discovery of gold in the Fraser turned Victoria and Fort Langley into boom towns. With the mainland suddenly much more attractive, fears of an American invasion grew and the colony's administrative centre was moved from Fort Langley, too close to enemy territory, to the more defensible Queensborough (later New Westminster). The city's governor, Colonel Moody, had defense, the Fraser's currents and the danger of freeze-up on his mind when he selected English Bay as an alternate anchorage in 1858. The following year, he set aside Stanley Park and land at Jericho and on the shore opposite the park as military reserves. His Royal Engineers began cutting trails that would later be major roads out to Queensborough's "back door": to Port Moody at the head of the inlet; to the head of False Creek and on to Jericho; down the Fraser to Point Grey; across to Burrard Inlet's Second Narrows.

Over the next five years, a handful of individuals settled at spots which would later become part of Vancouver. But neither their presence nor Moody's roads and military reserves provided the economic spark for future settlement. That came from the dense stands of fir and cedar that covered the land: from the lumber trade.

1887. Indian canoes on the Fraser River
near New Westminster. William Notman
photograph.

Sawdust & Skunk Cabbage 1860–1887

Vancouver's famous Stanley Park might now be covered with highrises if Captain Edward Stamp's first sawmill had succeeded, but the swift currents of the First Narrows made anchoring at the mill's wharf almost impossible, and Stamp was forced to move to the foot of Dunlevy where, in 1865, he built what became known as Hastings Mill, Vancouver's first industry. Although the mainland colony's land law of 1860 made the area available for settlement, it was really the opening of Stamp's second mill on 18 June 1867 that drew settlers; that, and the barrel of whiskey which Gassy Jack Deighton used to buy the help of the mill hands who built his Globe Saloon. Gastown got a jail in 1871, a post office in 1872, a school in 1873 and daily steamboat service to New Westminster in 1874. Still, well into the 1870s it was nothing more than a straggling line of buildings set in a damp, two-block clearing backed by rain forest. Boats were the only effective link with the outside. It was 1876 before a road joined Gastown and Hastings Townsite, near the Second Narrows, and it still took the better part of two days to reach Victoria.

The colony's older settlements could afford to sneer at Gastown, and did. In 1882, when Burrard Inlet was announced as the CPR terminus, Port Moody went wild with land speculation. Few besides CPR officials and Premier W.M. Smithe knew that secret negotiations would give Gastown the terminus in return for land grants to the company comprising modern Vancouver's central business district, right-of-way along north False Creek and a huge tract south of False Creek, including what is now Shaughnessy.

The CPR presence gave shape to the city which is Vancouver today. The company's land grants and its choice of the foot of Howe Street for its station and deep-sea wharves, and the corner of Georgia and Granville for its hotel, swung the centre of power and wealth to the city's west side, made way for the West End and Shaughnessy as posh residential districts, and dictated the future commercial dominance of Georgia and Granville.

Furor followed the public announcement of the new terminus. While the *Port Moody Gazette* carried vitriolic denunciations of the betrayal, speculators descended on Vancouver. Crosscut saws and dynamite extended the original clearing to the south and west. Hotels and houses multiplied: in February 1886 there were only 100 homes; by May, 600. Vancouver became a city on 6 April 1886, and as one of his first official acts, Mayor M.A. MacLean and his council sent a petition to the Dominion government requesting the grant of "The Reserve" (Stanley Park) to the city.

All spring, Vancouver residents had suffered the pall of smoke from burning slash. Then, on June 13, a sudden wind caught one of the clearing fires and sent a wall of flame over the town, killing at least 20 people and destroying everything but the Regina Hotel and the mill. Recovery was quick, spurred by the anticipation of the economic boom the railway would bring. By the end of 1886, the city boasted 14 offices, 23 hotels, 51 stores, 9 saloons, one church, one roller skating rink and over 8,000 people. Vancouver was ready for the train.

Top ca. 1867. In the woods at Burrard
Inlet. F. Dally photograph.

Bottom 1870. Water Street (known then
as Front Street) in Gastown. Ridley
photograph.

Old people say Indians see first whiteman up near Squamish. When they see first ship they think it an island with three dead trees....Indian braves in about twenty canoes come down Squamish river, go see. Get nearer, see men on island, men have black clothes with high hat coming to point at top.... Whitemans give Indians ship's biscuit; Indian not know what biscuit for. Before whitemans come Indians have little balls, not very big, roll them along ground, shoot at them with bow and arrow for practice, teach young Indian so as not to miss deer.... Indian not know ship's biscuit good to eat, so roll them along ground like little practice balls, shoot at them, break them up....

Then whitemans on schooner give molasses same time biscuit.... You know Indian sit on legs for long time in canoe; legs get stiff; rub molasses on legs make stiffness not so bad, molasses stick legs bottom of canoe. Molasses not much good for stiff legs, but my ancestors think so; not their fault; just mistake; they not know molasses good to eat.

August Jack Khahtsahlano, quoted in J.S. Matthews, *Early Vancouver*, volume 2, number 37.

A visit paid this week to the various mills and lumbering establishments on Burrard Inlet (our outer harbor) has tended to impress us more than ever with the magnitude and growing importance of our forest wealth, and to convince us that it is the imperative duty of the Government to afford every reasonable facility for the development of this almost inexhaustible resource. A pleasant drive of eight and a half miles ... brought us to the "Brighton Hotel," well kept by its enterprising owner, Mr. Oliver Hocking....

Embarking in a canoe with an Indian and his dusky spouse as a motive power, half an hour brought us to Captain Stamp's mills.... Proceeding across English Bay, a magnificent sheet of water, affording secure anchorage for the combined navies of the world, we found ourselves at Mr. Rogers' camp....

Mr. Rogers.... has now a contract from Captain Stamp for taking out three cargoes of spars for the French, Russian and Dutch Governments respectively.

from "Our Forest Wealth", *The British Columbian*, 13 October 1866.

1872. Hastings Sawmill and wharf.

ca. 1872. Moodyville, on the north shore
of Burrard Inlet. David Withrow
photograph.

There used to be a great fleet of vessels in Burrard Inlet sometimes. The most I ever remember was forty-two vessels all at one time; ships, barques, barquentines, brigs, brigantines, and three and four masted schooners; those three and four masted schooners were big vessels, too: that was at the time Captain Stamp had the mill (Hastings Mill); must have been around 1875, I suppose; they came from all parts of the world, some loading spars, some lumber, some shingles....

John H. Scales, quoted in J.S. Matthews, *Early Vancouver*, volume 3, number 33.

Scattered along the coast from the head of Johnstone Strait to Burrard Inlet were the shacks of scores of handloggers who cut timber on their own account and sold them to the mills after they had been scaled by the mill scaler. These men were usually in partnerships of two. Some of their dwellings, or shacks, were located in most picturesque spots, and were often hidden in the dense foliage which surrounded them, and their locality could only be divined by the chutes they built, on which the immense sticks glided into the water. For it must be remembered that in those days no logs were taken, or even looked at, which contained a knot to mar the beauty of the flooring into which much of it was cut. The trees cut down were generally those which had not a branch below sixty or seventy feet from the ground.... There was a great demand at this time for square timber of large size in China, and a great deal of it went there.

from W. Wymond Walkem, M.D., "Christmas Thirty-eight Years Ago", [1877], *Stories of Early British Columbia*, 1914.

In the old days it was the custom to have two gangs longshoring, and one was an Indian gang, and one a white gang, and each loaded their own side of the vessel. You see, if you stow more on one side than the other you get a list on the ship. The Indians would break their necks to beat the whites, and get a list on the ship towards their side; sometimes they beat the whites; that's why we did it that way.

Mr. R.H. Alexander, quoted in J.S. Matthews, *Early Vancouver*, volume 3, number 85.

Top ca. 1882. Royal City Mills logging camp in Kitsilano or West Point Grey.

Bottom Early loggers.

In 1885, a traveller on the then fast and commodious steamer Maude, from Victoria to Burrard Inlet, would observe on entering the Inlet on his right or south side, a few scatter[ed] buildings, along the shore line of the deep bay, then, as now, called Coal Harbor....

To reach this place of possibly 150 inhabitants the traveller was obliged to disembark at the wharf at Hastings mill, about half a mile east of the village, and from there thread his way as best he could along a narrow trail, through dense timber to the only places of public accomodation to be then found on Burrard Inlet....

This place in 1872 had been surveyed and platted as a townsite and a few lots ... had been sold.... But so little was thought of the situation and prospects that only about thirteen lots were bought.

from "Vancouver City", Souvenir Edition, *The Vancouver Daily World*, 1890.

Many a night, as I lay in bed in my front room in the Tom Cyrs' Granville Hotel on Water Street, I have heard the deer's hoofs go tap, tap, tap, on the board sidewalk beneath.

George Cary, quoted in J.S. Matthews, *Early Vancouver*, volume 2, number 191.

There were practically no white children born on Burrard Inlet; about the only births were Indian births; white women expecting confinement went to Victoria. You see, there was not a doctor nearer than New Westminster, and to reach New Westminster it was necessary, first, to send a message by an Indian and his canoe to Maxie's at the "End of the Road" — as we used to call it (Hastings) — about three miles by water, and then a horseman had to ride to New Westminster over the old Douglas Road; it was almost a twelve hour journey to get there, find the doctor and return.

Mrs. Alice Crakanthorp, quoted in J.S. Matthews, *Early Vancouver*, volume 4, number 149.

Top Hastings Sawmill.

Centre 1885. Hastings Sawmill cottage.

Bottom 11 June 1886. Hastings Mill school two days before the fire.

Burns was a whiteman married to my sister Louisa, and, after he die, they "kick" her out; he had a six acre orchard there [Jerry's Cove]. But that's the way they do with Indian womans who marries whiteman; when their husband dies, they kick the womans out — because she's "just a squaw."

August Jack Khahtsahlano, quoted in J.S. Matthews, *Early Vancouver*, volume 4, page 44.

When "Gassy Jack" had the sole [saloon] licence he was very dictatorial and would turn out the lights and his customers at 10:30, with a reminder that they had to sleep that they might work for him on the morrow, which they mostly did, as the bulk of their wages used to find their way into Jack's coffers. But when more licences were granted this custom changed, and I have known our mill shut down for a couple of days because so many were engaged in a particularly interesting game that was going on.

from R.H. Alexander, "Reminiscences of the Early Days of B.C.", *The Canadian Club of Vancouver: Addresses and Proceedings: 1910-11*, 23 February 1911.

One New Year's Eve — everybody called on everybody on New Year's Eve in those days — "Rusty" Pleace was "half shot," so they wheeled him around with them on their visits in a wheel barrow, but finally they got tired of wheeling him, so they tied him up to the old Maple Tree at Gastown with a horse chain; he was still there in the morning.

Harold E. Ridley, quoted in J.S. Matthews, *Early Vancouver*, volume 3, page 78.

Thank God for having brought us safely thro' the *first* year of our stay here. Never spent a year more barren seemingly of results and more uncongenial to my tastes and sympathies. My soul is oft tried by the surrounding vice and profligacy. May the good Lord keep me and my dear family from the evil power of the enemy. Thank God for the manifold mercies of the year!

from the diary of Cornelius Bryant, [preacher for the Canadian Methodist Church], July 1879, additional MS. 24, Vancouver City Archives.

1884. Wah Chong Chinese laundry on the south side of Water Street between Abbott and Carrall streets.

ca. 1884. Gastown waterfront.
From the left, the Sunnyside Hotel,
George Black's house and butcher
shop, the Granville Hotel and other
businesses and homes.

THE GEM CIGAR DIVAN

CORDOVA STREET

SMOKERS' GOODS,

TO SUIT ALL TASTES

DOMESTIC & IMPORTED SMOKING

CIGARS A SPECIALTY

JACK LEVY

13

St. James Parish came into being as a mission district centering around Gastown or the old Granville townsite....

The naming of the church was an unconscious expression of mother-love. At an informal gathering which included the Bishop, Cpt. and Mrs. Raymur, Mr. Ditcham, the choice of a name was under discussion. "Call it St. James, after our Jimmy," suggested Mrs. Raymur.

from notes by Rev. George Ditcham, c. 1881, Anglican Archives, UBC.

On both sides of the inlet, those who were not connected with the camps spent their Christmas much as they do now. Plum puddings and mince pies engaged the attention of the busy housewives for weeks in advance of the festive occasion. Isolated to a certain extent from the rest of British Columbia, a social and sympathetic feeling bound all as though in one family bond. Go into any house where there were children, and your ears were greeted with squeaking trumpets and hammering of drums, and even before you reached the door the evidence that Santa Claus had not forgotten the little children of this far western harbor was before your eyes in sleighs being pulled on sawdust and mud, or skates being tested on the same material.

from W. Wymond Walkem, M.D., "Christmas Thirty-eight Years Ago", [1877], Stories of Early British Columbia, 1914.

Vancouver, unlike other cities, has as yet no popular places of resort, or pleasant strolls into the country.... During the past summer our harbor has been made the resort on which a great many have spent pleasantly the few leisure hours at their disposal.... This practice has been looked upon by some as a violation of the law of God, and who favor prohibiting the renting of boats and the running of excursions on that day.... Surely it was never meant that our young men and women should, after a hard week's work confine themselves exclusively to attending religious services and reading religious books.... Fresh air and freedom from care are as essential to health as the food we eat, and until Vancouver can boast of its parks and boarded avenues, we see no other resource than the water.

from "Observing the Sabbath", The Daily News-Advertiser, 12 September 1886.

Top 1886. St. James Church near Main (known as Westminster at the time) and Alexander streets. H.T. Devine photograph.

Bottom 24 May 1886. Boating on Seymour Creek on the north side of Burrard Inlet. H.T. Devine photograph.

February 1886. Clearing at
approximately Hastings Street and
Westminster Avenue (now Main Street).

Lately we have changed our name from the pleasing one of Granville, for this bombastic swaggering title of Vancouver. It is called this because it is to be the terminus of the great Canadian Pacific Railway.... However all the swagger in the world will not build houses, and if they don't mend soon they will have this place a city of shanties, without water, roads or drains.... The roads are quite impassable from the mudholes till this week when a lot of glorious weather has improved matters, though still leaving some awful mud holes, so bad that even a short legged man on horse-back can hardly keep his feet out of the mud.... The water here that folk drink (when they do drink water) is all surface water, in other words drainage, but still the doctors all four of them are in despair, and in bitter disappointment cry out in chorus, "No typhoid yet."

from a letter by Father Clinton, 3 April 1886, additional MS. 192, Vancouver City Archives.

After the first council meeting civic organization was, more or less, complete, but there was no money in the treasury, and the question of finances came up early.... Some money was collected from fines inflicted on disorderly or drunket persons, but they were very small amounts, two dollars and fifty cents, went to pay the police salaries....

W.H. Gallagher, quoted in J.S. Matthews, *Early Vancouver*, volume 1, number 296.

I cannot say that I am pleased with the original planning of Vancouver; the work was beset with many difficulties; the dense forest, the inlet on the north, the creek on the south, a registered plan on the east, another on the west, and old Granville in the centre.... I planned all the streets leading westernly (from Burrard street) so that they would run without a jog, but one owner determined to fight in the courts to prevent any change in the registered plan, and I was able to give continuous line on alternate streets only.... The corner post, with nail in centre of top, from which the survey of Vancouver commenced, was planted with a certain amount of ceremony at the corner of Hastings and Hamilton streets.

L.A. Hamilton, quoted in J.S. Matthews, *Early Vancouver*, volume 2, number 191.

Top August 1886. Hastings Hotel at Hastings Townsite just west of the second narrows of Burrard Inlet. The town had a bathing beach and was a popular summer resort. J.A. Brock photograph.

Bottom May 1886. Maple Tree Square, corner of Carrall and Water streets, looking south on Carrall. H.T. Devine photograph.

One huge flame, a hundred feet long, burst from the Deighton Hotel, leaped "Maple Tree Square", and swallowed up the buildings where now stands the Europe Hotel; the fire went down the old "Hastings Road" (Alexander street) faster than a man could run. Two iron tires and some ashes were all that was left of man, horse, and cart which perished in the middle of Carrall street.

William F. Findlay, quoted in J.S. Matthews, *Early Vancouver*, volume 2, number 185.

...we then crossed nearly as far as Pender Street where the fire met us like a wall. Our clothes commenced to burn and our handkerchiefs dried up like chips. We were just about to give up when I noticed a small gravel patch. I proposed to lie down and see if the fire would pass over us, so Boultbee, Bailey, the stranger, and myself, lay flat on the gravel, which was not very hot at the time.

To the westward side a large frame house was burning, and it was so near that the burning timber came falling about us, causing us agonies that I cannot describe. Bailey could not stand this and said he was going to get through at any cost, but he could not penetrate a foot in the flames, and after running around for a few seconds, he dropped and burned up before our eyes.

from C. Gardner Johnson, *Romance of Vancouver*, 1926.

We were at Moodyville, and I just went out to get the pudding for dinner, and looking out of the door I saw the terrific smoke coming from Gastown; such a terrific smoke. And then I saw the steamers coming out.... We went down to see them land; it was tragic to see the people come ashore; their shoes were charred.... The people were taken to the hotel at Moodyville and served with supper... and when bedtime came they were taken to the Masonic Hall.... It was pitiful to see them sleeping. The people were all very tired, and very quiet. Some had just the clothing they wore, nothing else, and many did not know where their children were; it was very, very pitiful.

Mrs. Alice Crakanthorp, quoted in J.S. Matthews, *Early Vancouver*, volume 4, page 157.

16 June 1886. City Hall in a tent. H.T. Devine photograph.

Top left 14 June 1886. The day after the fire. H.T. Devine photograph.

Bottom left 14 June 1886. Refugee tents at the south end of the False Creek Bridge near Front Street and Westminster Avenue (now 1st Avenue and Main Street).

1886. Cordova Street looking west from
Carrall Street, five weeks after the fire.

Mr. Strathie was rebuilding when I arrived; a two storey home ... on our old leased lot on Water street; the floor was down, the scantling of the frame was up, and part of the siding, perhaps three or four feet, but there was no roof. The Hastings Mill was but a small mill in those days... but when the great demand for lumber for re-building Vancouver was thrown upon them it was beyond their capacity to meet it, so that the lumber was apportioned out, and that was the reason so little progress had been made, during my seven days absence, in the construction of our house.

Mrs. Emily Strathie, quoted in J.S. Matthews, *Early Vancouver*, volume 2, number 207.

You cannot imagine any place rougher and more disagreeable in appearance than Vancouver itself as it is covered with burnt logs and stumps and not a green thing to be seen. You will understand this when I tell you it was a perfect wilderness on the first of last April and the ground has been cleared since....

The principal difference [between Vancouver and the East] is in the cost of servants — wages of a cook (Chinese) being $25 and white $30 to $40 per month. Beef is 12½ cents a lb. and mutton about the same as in Brockville and groceries are about the same as in Montreal, perhaps a shade higher.

from H. Abbott to S. Campbell Sweeney, 9 August 1886, additional MS. 22, Vancouver City Archives.

The plans for the water supply of Vancouver are about completed, and Chief Engineer G.A. Keefer, assisted by Mr. H.B. Smith, has just finished the final survey, locating the point of supply on the Capilano River.... The source of supply is fed by glaciers, and, running over a granite bed, makes it the purest to be obtained under any circumstances.... The water will be conveyed on the bed of Burrard Inlet in mains, entering the city at its western limits and running through the principal streets to the eastern limits.

from "The City's Water Supply", *The Vancouver News*, 5 August 1886.

Top July 1886. SS "Princess Louise" at the Hastings Mill Store wharf on the foot of Dunlevy Avenue.

Bottom 16 June 1886. The first quarters of the Tremont Hotel after the original building was destroyed in the fire.

GRANVILLE HOTEL,

Granville, Burrard Inlet.

Newly Built
and Newly Furnished,

Large and Commodious.

The roller skating rink opens for the first time on Saturday evening at 7 o'clock.

from "Echoes of the Streets", *The Vancouver News*, 23 July 1886.

No owner or driver of any open cab shall drive, or suffer, or permit to be driven, about the streets of said city during the daytime, in any such open cab, any notoriously bad characters, or women of ill-fame, unless for the purpose of taking such person to or from the railway station, or wharf, or steamboat landing.

from By-law number 11, 13 August 1886.

Any person or persons, firm or corporate body whatsoever, who shall manufacture, sell, barter, exchange, or in any manner whatsoever traffic in or with opium in any form (except a duly qualified chemist or druggist, and then only on a physician's prescription) whether crude or manufactured, or either, within the corporate limits of the City of Vancouver, shall be subject to and shall first pay a licence fee or duty of $500 p.a., to be payable half-yearly in advance on the 1st day of July and the 1st day of January of each year....

from By-law number 160, 13 August 1886.

Allow me to remind the users of steam whistles that their excessive use at unreasonable hours is an unmitigated nuisance. This morning between 4:45 and 6 one whistle indulged in ten prolonged ear-splitting screams disturbing the whole city from its reasonable slumbers. The probable intention was to call some half-dozen men to their work. But why disturb a whole town? Kindly be more moderate.
    Yours etc.,
    T.C. Sorby

from *The Daily News-Advertiser*, 7 September 1886.

The first hospital, was at the foot of Hawks Avenue; in the angle of Alexander and Powell St. It ... consisted, in April, 1886, when I came, of a small wooden building and some tents. There were a lot of accidents during construction days....

W.H. Gallagher, quoted in J.S. Matthews, *Early Vancouver*, volume 1, number 302.

McDougall had conceived the idea of subbing this work to Chinamen and did so, this is what led up to the "Chinese" riots of the fall and winter of '86 and '87, and got John the sobriquet of Chinese McDougall. The R.R. work was mostly all done and Vancouver was full of men, some out of work, and some not wanting work. This element took exception to Chinese doing the clearing, and under the guidance of a good intentioned old gent by the name of "Pitt", these men held indignation meetings and took it upon their shoulders to send the Chinamen back to Victoria, where they came from, and at the same time, declaring Vancouver was to be a non-Chinese city. Well, they rounded up the celestials with no great care. I can see the picture yet, of these poor chinks with their rice sacks and big baskets and balancing poles, all heading for the wharf; they were coming out of the blackened timber and brush from all directions, and some of them were coming on the toe of a boot. They were herded on the wharf ... and sent back again to Victoria; then the powers at Victoria (who were at that time jealous of the young upstart-town of Vancouver) clapped on the screws, placing Vancouver under Martial Law, and the Chinamen finished the contract in the end.

George H. Keefer, quoted in J.S. Matthews, *Early Vancouver*, volume 4, page 385.

Oh! sad is the fate of Vancouver,
Its sweet little game's about over,
I said from the *First*
The bubble would burst
And astonish the dupes of Vancouver.

   . . . .

To save them from sheer desolation
Let us offer them some consolation
Before they get broody,
Invite them to Moody,
And thus end their great consternation.

from "The Injunctions", *The Port Moody Gazette*, 28 August 1886.

STEAM TO CARIBOO !

The *British Columbia* GENERAL TRANSPORTATION COMPANY

Will place Four of THOMSON'S PATENT ROAD STEAMERS on the route between Yale and Barkerville in the First Week in April, and will be prepared to enter into Contracts for the conveyance of Freight from Yale to Soda Creek in EIGHT DAYS. Through Contracts will be made as soon as the condition of the road above Quesnelmouth permits.
Rates of Passage will be advertised in due time.

BARNARD & BEEDY, managers.

DOUGLAS PINE TREES, VANCOUVER

Terminal City
1887–1900

On 23 May 1887, when the first through passenger train pulled into the CPR's new Howe Street station, Vancouver's isolation ceased. It became a crucial link in the British Empire's "All Red Route": the end of a national railway and the Canadian deep-sea port for Oriental trade. Three weeks later, the *Abyssinia* arrived with passengers and tea from Japan. Four years later the CPR's famous Empresses began regular passenger service to the Orient.

From the broad verandahs of the first Hotel Vancouver, visitors looked down on a growing city. Plans to replace well water with water from the Capilano River system, brought by pipe under the First Narrows, were going ahead. The 1889 city directory proudly recorded twenty miles of graded streets and — a mark of civilization — six miles of planked sidewalks. In public transit, Vancouver opted for the day's leading technology: an electric street car system, perfected only a year earlier in Richmond, Virginia. The first tiny cars began service in 1890 and within two years an extension of the line across False Creek on the new Granville Bridge brought settlement to Mount Pleasant and Fairview. The interurban line between Vancouver and New Westminster opened in 1891, allowing settlement at Grandview and Cedar Cottage.

The CPR had already cut Granville Street through from Burrard Inlet to the north arm of the Fraser. Carbon arc lamps shone down on the major streets, and picnickers at English Bay could call home on the area's first pay telephone. The city took its place on Canada's cultural map in 1891, when the CPR's new Opera House opened with a performance of Wagner's *Lohengrin*. Two years later, the Hudson's Bay Company opened a store at the still out-of-the-way location of Georgia and Granville.

Now that Vancouver was linked to the rest of the world, it suffered the world's troubles. A smallpox epidemic struck in 1892, probably spread from sailors on the Empresses. The economic depression which began in 1892-93 hit Vancouver along with the rest of the continent. That and the disastrous Fraser Valley flood of 1894 brought hundreds of refugees and washed-out loggers to Vancouver's soup kitchens. When the Klondike gold rush came in 1897, the overflow business Vancouver picked up from Victoria and Seattle was a welcome relief.

As the city proudly sent seventeen men off to fight for Britain's cause against the Boers in 1899, the economy was again stronger. Yet even into the last years of the century, this city of contrasts, a city whose people enjoyed modern conveniences and technology, but lived in the midst of wilderness and half-cleared land, remained relatively compact. In 1897, 80 per cent of the city's 20,000 people still lived within a mile of the CPR station. Going downtown meant only a twenty-minute walk. Shortly after the turn of the century this would change as the city began its second major period of growth.

From early morning yesterday it was easy to see that some unusual occurrence was about to take place. The streets were covered with people many in holiday costumes walking around watching the work of decorating.... The buildings ... along the principal streets were decorated with evergreens, flags, bunting etc., while from every flagmast in the city a flag of some nationality was flying out before the breeze.... All the ships in the harbor were decked out in all colors....

The scene at the station was a very lively and enthusiastic one, the roadway, wharf, platform and the bank above were covered with people waiting the arrival of the train....

At 12:45 while all were straining their eyes eastwards, the loud whistle of the engine was heard, "here she comes"! "here she comes"! was heard on all sides and at the same time a rush for the platform was made by those on the banks above. A minute later amidst the cheers of the people, ringing of bells and the shrill cry of the locomotive whistle, the first through passenger train entered the station and pulled up in Vancouver.

from "Ocean to Ocean", *The Daily News-Advertiser*, 24 May 1887.

The C.P.R. opened up and rough graded, all at their own expense, a number of the streets west of Cambie Street; they had no interests east of Cambie Street. The summer of the fire, 1886, they opened up and rough graded Cordova St., Hastings St., Pender St., all west of Cambie St., and, in the spring of 1887, opened up Granville Street from water to water, from the Inlet to False Creek. They did not clear it the full sixty-six feet, but made a passable road leaving the stumps on both sides. From Burrard Inlet to the Hotel Vancouver they laid down a good planked driveway, ten or twelve feet wide....

Later the C.P.R. opened up what is now known as Granville Street South, clear through from False Creek to the Fraser River at the North Arm; of course, it ran through their own land.

W.H. Gallagher, quoted in J.S. Matthews, *Early Vancouver*, volume 1, number 302.

Page 22 1887. First Hotel Vancouver. William Notman photograph.

Left 23 May 1887. Arrival of the first through passenger train in the CPR station at the north foot of Howe Street. H.T. Devine photograph.

Top ca. 1889. View of the CPR station and "The Bluff" above, where railroad officials built their homes.

Bottom ca. 1887. Looking west from Jackson Avenue and Hastings Street. The Hotel Vancouver is in the background near the tall trees.

Top ca. 1890. R.V. Winch Fruit and Game Store. C.S. Bailey and Co. photograph.

Bottom ca. 1890. Butcher shop.

An eastern man's first question when thinking of coming to Vancouver is, "What is your climate?" On this side of the range of mountains that skirt the coast from north to south at varying distances, the climate is such that fuchsias will thrive the year round. Snow rarely lies more than a day or two at a time, with the possible exception of the past winter, even which was not severe enough to inconvenience anyone to any degree. During the summer, the sultry and oppressive weather prevalent in the east is unknown here, and while occasionally the mercury reaches 85°, there is never a night in the year when one cannot sleep under a blanket. The city has its occasional visitations of fogs, which moderate the climate, and give needed moisture to vegetation. From a sanitary point of view, there is not a more invigorating region in the whole province than Vancouver. Here, in common with all parts of the coast, there are but two seasons, wet and dry, which may account in a measure for the entire absence of many diseases prevalent in corresponding latitudes elsewhere. Sunstroke and prostration from heat are unknown, and the ratio of deaths from pulmonary complaints is notably small.

from Williams' *Vancouver and New Westminster Cities Directory*, 1890.

Those were the *busiest* times, so much entertaining, so many dances, so difficult to get help in the household. White help at any price was almost impossible, and the Chinamen were so independent; if there was an extra person for dinner, or something the Chinaman did not like, they would pack up and walk out without saying a word.

Mrs. Malcolm A. MacLean, quoted in J.S. Matthews, *Early Vancouver*, volume 2, number 231.

Oh, we never saw shoes from June 'til September. Soon as school was out we'd lose our shoes right away.... We used to have lots of fun in our bare feet, specially when the road would be dusty and the watering carts would come along; [it] was a lovely chance to get out on the road and make mud pies with our toes.

from an interview with J. Rodger Burnes, number 175, [ca. 1900], Oral History Programme, Reynoldston Research and Studies.

Winter 1887. Cordova Street looking east from Abbott Street.

GOD · SAVE · OUR · QUEEN

1837   1887

Vancouver's · Jubilee · Celebration

— OF THE —

Fiftieth Anniversary of The Reign of
Her Most Gracious Majesty

Queen : Victoria

FRIDAY & SATURDAY
JULY 1st & 2nd, '87

Vancouver in 1889 presented curious contrasts. Take Granville Street, for instance, in which we were living. One end led to the docks, with 3,000 ton steamers lying in them, and the terminus of a transcontinental railway; the other left you at the end of a bridge which led to the forest, and, after miles of mud, to New Westminster.... The extraordinary thing about Vancouver is that in the midst of all this wilderness it is so absolutely modern; no one would think of putting up a house without a telephone and electric light.

from Douglas Sladen, "On the Cars and Off", London.

Back in 1890 the late B.T. Rogers, then a young man, arrived in Vancouver for the purpose of starting a sugar refinery. Having selected the site, he now approached the city council in the old city hall on Powell Street for some concessions. He asked for free water for a certain period and some exemptions from taxation and in return therefore to establish an industry giving employment to a hundred persons.

At that time sawmills and canneries were about the only large concerns operating, and these mostly employed Chinese. I was delegated by the Trades and Labor Council to watch the case on behalf of labor. Getting permission from Mayor Oppenheimer to speak I opposed any concessions to any industry unless white men were to be employed. Mr. Rogers protested he had no intention of employing any other.

from William Fleming, "Memories of Early Vancouver — The Sugar Refinery and Chinese", additional MS. 132, Vancouver City Archives.

Never in our history have there been better opportunities for Profitable and Safe Investment than the present, as the City is now being whipped into shape, and the centre is being established....Invest now and thus avoid wailing over lost opportunities.

from *The Daily News-Advertiser*, advertisement, 7 November 1888.

Top 1889. Laying the first streetcar tracks on Powell Street between Heatley and Princess avenues.

Bottom 1 July 1890. Parade on Cordova Street. H.T. Devine photograph.

1890. Bathing beauties.

Well Kept Lawns
Should be Well
Rolled Lawns

No person shall bathe or swim in the waters of Burrard Inlet or English Bay within the City limits between the hours of 6 o'clock in the forenoon and 8 o'clock in the evening without a bathing dress covering the body from the neck to the knees, and any person wearing such proper bathing dress may bathe at any time in the waters of Burrard Inlet or English Bay within the City limits.

from By-law number 135, 17 March 1892.

All the summer occupations and amusements have wakened up once more. Both rowing clubs are at it every night in anticipation of regattas on the 11th and 21st instant, in one of which yours truly is to take part and for which he has placed himself every night at the tender mercies of a 'stroke' for about the past two weeks. Then the cricketers are looking out their flannels, the lacrosse men have arranged their matches, and there is a vague whisper of pic-nics in the air, the first of which will probably come off on the 24th of May, which is a great day with Canadians.

from F.M. Black, letter to Dr. Craig, 5 May 1892, B.C. Provincial Archives.

The tennis sash is meeting with favor rather slowly.

Fancy vests of tennis cloth, marseilles, cheviot and flannel are much worn.

Black ball buttons for white vests can be seen in some of the furnishing stores.

Something novel for the tourist is a tobacco pouch in the shape of a fish made of rubber.

There is a prediction among the tailors that light colored doeskin trousers will be introduced next fall.

Trousers show a slight decrease in size. Nineteen and a half at the knee and eighteen at the bottom are the proper dimensions.

from "Fashions for Men", *The Vancouver Daily World*, 16 January 1890.

The race track was on Howe Street; it must have started about Nelson Street and ended about the Hotel Vancouver; I think the grand stand must have been where the hotel stands; it was a long affair. Everybody went to the races.

from J.S. Matthews, *Early Vancouver*, volume 1, number 23.

31

The bicycle became so popular that racks were put up in the vestibules of the small office buildings to receive the 'machines' of those employed there and who had business there.... At the corner of Pender and Granville street, where now stands the Rogers Building, a school for bicycle riding was flourishing. It covered two or three lots ... and [was] fenced with a high fence — to hide it from the curious, for pupils did not take kindly to making a public amusement for street spectators by their efforts to stay on a 'wheel'.

from J.S. Matthews, *Early Vancouver*, volume 1, number 107.

Twenty-five live and 300 lbs. of dressed turkeys to be shot for and raffled off at the shooting gallery tonight, 204 Carrall Street. All lovers of sport invited.

from *The Vancouver Daily World*, 21 December 1893.

People at the railway station when the Pacific Express arrived yesterday were astonished to see two ladies seated upon the cow catcher of the engine. They had occupied that dangerous position from North Bend to Vancouver, their desire to see the scenery along the line overcoming their fondness for the greater comfort but less advantageous position of the observation car or sleeper. These ladies also passed over the greater part of the line from Banff to Revelstoke on the same rather dangerous conveyance. They are English ladies on a visit to Canada and the United States.

from "The City", *The Daily News-Advertiser*, 2 August 1891.

My mother, very conservative, never had coloured or scented soap: pure white castile. And for the first time, in the C.P.R. washroom I discovered Pears delightfully scented soap. Well, when the tedium of the journey was urging me I would rise and take myself to the washroom and lather generously with Pears soap. Then I would go back to my seat and I could smell this delightful Pears soap and all through my life Pears soap, especially the well-scented, has been for me a bringer-back of romantic experience.

from an interview with Mrs. McQueen, number 156, [1891], Oral History Programme, Reynoldston Research and Studies.

Top ca. 1890. Wedding group.

Centre Sleigh by the Hollow Tree in Stanley Park.

Bottom Early 1890s. Even ladies took part in the bicycle craze.

1890. Panorama taken
from the Donald Smith Block
showing Granville Street on the right,
the Manor House Hotel on Howe and
Dunsmuir streets, and Stanley Park and
the north shore in background.

All interested should bear in mind that a meeting will be held in *The World* office on Tuesday afternoon at 3 o'clock to arrange for the distribution of *The World*'s Poor Children's Christmas Cheer Fund. Every church and contributing society is asked to send a delegate. Be on time and bring a list of all the poor families you know of with you. Do not expect to have a carriage sent round — that would be a waste of the fund's money: but come on time.

from "Children's Fund Meeting", *The Vancouver Daily World*, 19 December 1892.

Claude Kelly was yesterday found in a shack at English Bay, suffering from starvation and scurvy. He was immediately removed to the city hospital, where everything possible is being done for him. His discovery, and the preceding one of the man Hugh Ross have only served to emphasize the fact that unless destitute people are sufficiently diseased to be admitted to the city hospital, the civic authorities have no power to render them assistance in any way.... It has been suggested — and it is a wise suggestion too — that the charter revision committee would do well to have the laws of the city so amended that there should be a fund at the disposal of the Chief Magistrate from which to give relief in cases of absolute destitution, where such a deplorable condition is not brought on by the person's own misconduct. As the charter stands at present, a person may await death from starvation and the city may not be able to lend him a helping hand except by arresting him as a vagrant and sentencing him to a term of imprisonment.

from "The Jail as a Refuge", *The Vancouver Daily World*, 3 February 1893.

You have no idea how indifferent you will feel toward the coal combine if you buy your underwear at Dunlap, Cooke & Co.

from *The Vancouver Daily World*, 13 December 1892.

Top left 1890. Interior of the Secord Hotel, on the northeast corner of Powell Street and Dunlevy Avenue.

Bottom left 1890. Bachelor's Hall.

Top 1890. Manor House Hotel. Later the building became a boarding house called The Badminton.

Bottom 24 May 1887. Sunnyside Hotel decorated for Queen Victoria's birthday and the arrival of the train.

Top 1899. Indians camping after salmon fishing on waterfront along Alexander Street between Main and Columbia streets.

Bottom ca. 1898. Indian group on Alexander Street beach near the foot of Columbia Street. Thomas H. Moore photograph.

Around the city of Vancouver many excellent sites for camp can be secured. On Greer's Beach, outside the entrance to False Creek, many hundreds encamp during the summer on the level stretch of land just above the water's edge, with a grand sweep of sand at low tide. Others travel further out into English Bay and select a site on the high ground on the south side....

No time is lost on arrival, and a selected number of the party with axes and cross-cut saws start in and soon effect a clearance large enough to admit of the dining-tent, twenty-two feet by thirty feet, being run up. Into this we put all our available property, passed up, hand to hand, from the beach below....

On the following morning we are early astir and the work of clearing is renewed. By breakfast time as many as six fresh tents have been erected, and our canvas colony is assuming fair dimensions.... Many of the tents are floored with fir planks secured at a trifling cost at the logging camp, or boarded round with cedar shakes, by which not a little extra comfort is gained.... In the end a substantial fir railing is run around the cliff, rustic and other seats are set up, and our township is complete. Having by now thoroughly and conscientiously earned a respite from labour, both manual and physical, we disport ourselves as fancy dictates.

from W.J. Kerslake Flinton, "Camping Out in British Columbia", *The Windsor Magazine*, October, 1899.

I think that cows ought to be kept from running in the streets. I had a large field of cabbages in the east end of the city and a cow got in and spoilt them all and knocked down the fence.
A Prominent Citizen
P.S. I don't think I will sign my name as I do not wish to make bad friends with anybody.
A Citizen
(The above letter is inserted on account of the importance of the subject although the writer did not comply with the rules and enclose his name and address. —Ed.)
from *The Daily News-Advertiser*, 19 July 1888.

Is there anything more difficult or wearisome than to try and hold up a heavy skirt when in one hand you have an umbrella and in the other an array of small parcels? Never was there a time when a suitable rainy day costume was more necessary for the gentler sex than it is at present, for in taking her place beside man in the bread-winning contest of life, woman must inevitably subject herself to certain changes if she would attain success and one of these changes is a radical, rational one in dress. There are hundreds of girls to-day in Vancouver whom the exigencies of business or professional life take out in all kinds of weather, such for instance as type-writers, shopgirls and those employed in the multitudinous public occupations now open to women.

from *The Vancouver Semi-Weekly World*, 3 May 1898.

The large arch erected by the decoration committee across the foot of Granville Street fell yesterday afternoon with a loud crash during the prevalence of the stiff breeze that blew up from the south west about 4 o'clock. A man who was passing at the time had a very narrow escape, one of his cheeks being scratched by a piece of evergreen that decorated the arch.

from "First Arches in Vancouver", *The Daily News-Advertiser*, 8 July 1888.

A serious runaway on Hastings Street by a team of horses and a truck smashed a hydrant at Homer Street, flooded a basement, pulled down B.C. Electric trolley lines, knocked over a telephone pole and broke a bystander's leg. The driver was uninjured.

from "Forty Years Ago Today", *The Vancouver Sun*, 26 September 1938.

A man with a bundle of goods and apparently sober, attracted a large crowd to-day by his strange behaviour, dancing, kicking up and laughing boisterously. Some one said he would be apt to have a fit. He said there was no danger, that he had just had a good one in a pair of trousers he got at Russell, McDonald and Co's, and what made him feel so jolly was the how cheap he got them.

from "Local Brevities", *The Vancouver Daily World*, 8 April 1893.

Top ca. 1892. David Oppenheimer and friends on the Moodyville and Brockton Point ferry, leaving the City Wharf at the foot of Carrall Street. William Notman photograph.

Bottom 1896. Group of campers on Greer's (Kitsilano) Beach.

WM. RALPH'S,

24 CORDOVA St.

If a child is thin, let him take a little of Scott's emulsion of codliver oil. Some children like it too well, begin with a little. A half or quarter teaspoon is enough at first if the stomach is weak; but increase as you find the stomach will bear.

The effect is: the little one takes on strength, gets hungry; eats and is happy; gets fat — he ought to be fat — and gets healthy.

from Scott & Bowne, Chemists, Toronto, advertisement, *The Vancouver Province*, 14 November 1900.

There is no doubt that the electric light wire is dangerous — that it has killed a great many people. A good deal of the outcry on this account, however, is raised by electric-lighting companies themselves, each asserting that the apparatus of its rival is very deadly. Gas company officials join in and affirm that all of them are very deadly. The situation is not dissimilar to that of half a century ago, when railways began to supplant stage coaches. But notwithstanding frequent appalling accidents, we now know that railway traveling is much less dangerous than traveling by coach. It will be so with electric lighting.

from "They Are Dangerous", *The Vancouver Daily World*, 14 January 1890.

I call to mind when we were consider[ing] a proposal to have the City Hall lighted by electricity. The company soliciting the business, installed a 16 candle power light. Alderman Humphreys, much opposed to any new fangled notions, was prepared to squash the proposal. When the light was turned on, much to my enjoyment, Alderman Humphreys produced from under the table, where he was sitting, a common tallow candle, and striding forward to the centre electric light, struck a match on his pants, lit the candle, and then proudly holding it up to the electric lamp, said, "Mr. Mayor, they call this thing that they want to plant on us 16 candle power; I call it a swindle. I don't see any improvement in it over this common single candle." (great applause with a certain section) However, in spite of this demonstration we went ahead and made the contract.

L.A. Hamilton, quoted in J.S. Matthews, *Early Vancouver*, volume 4, page 300.

A lecture by Mr. W. Vemilgea, President of the Phrenological Society will be given this evening in the Young Men's Christian Association. The subject will be "Character in the Head and Face", and during the evening several public examinations will be made. All are welcome.

from "The City", *The Daily News-Advertiser*, 16 January 1897.

Having travelled through from Great Britain to your beautiful City, I was much struck by the rapid growth of Manitoba and the North West Territories.... But at Calgary I was almost dumb-folded, when I saw a play bill from your City announcing Sarah Bernhardt for two nights at the Vancouver Opera House; the idol of Paris, the rage of London, playing in a city of five years growth, seemed to me almost an impossibility until I arrived in your City and saw your magnificent Opera House; an Opera House I can safely say second to none in Great Britain.... Well done Vancouver, your businessmen show a great spirit that must soon bring your City to the fore on this great Pacific Coast.

Your truly,

George Willoughby, Crofton House Fareham, Hants.

from *The Daily News-Advertiser*, 16 September 1891.

The aggregation of stale jokes, cracked voices and horse-play has paid us its annual visit. A large number of people attended the performance last night, although the alarming sounds of the brass band during the street parade might well have warned them away. However, they went, and they paid a dollar, some of them! It would be interesting to hear how they felt about that dollar this morning — interesting, but possibly not edifying. The Gorton Minstrel troupe is only fit to play down in some ten-cent house where the audience can smoke and enjoy itself and pay no attention to the stage.

from "Footlight Flashes", *The Vancouver Daily World*, 25 October 1899.

Wanted — Thirty men without mustaches and 20 ladies Tuesday evening for La Tosca. Apply to Business Manager, Opera House.

from *The Vancouver Daily World*, 21 September 1891.

We went over to Vancouver once in a while, driving up Granville Street, as it is now called, but then it was just a slit in the forest; a solid wall of trees on both sides from Eburne to False Creek with timber so tall you had to look straight up to see the sky. We went over to Vancouver on the first day of July, 1890, and the mud on Granville Street was up to the hubs. The sun could not get in to dry the road — the trees were so tall. The road was no wider than a wagon, and, every half mile or so, there was a little space, somewhat wider, where wagons could pass.

Mrs. H.E. Campbell, quoted in J.S. Matthews, *Early Vancouver*, volume 1, number 152.

Then, when they put the Capilano water in, at first they just gave us a tap out at the front of the house.... Then, when the sewer came, we put in the sink, and, after a time when we could afford it we put in the bath; before that we used a great big tub — a huge thing of wooden staves about twenty-four inches high — and bathed in front of the kitchen stove; it was quite a "business" on a Saturday night where there were four or five youngsters.

Mrs. Burns, quoted in J.S. Matthews, *Early Vancouver*, volume 4, page 108.

Nearly all the lanes improved during 1896 have been done by the chaingang under officer North. The work has always been promptly and well done and the officer in charge of the chaingang is to be commended for the good judgement shown in the execution of the work. The estimated value of the work done by the chaingang this year is $2,966.

from "Annual Report of the Chairman of the Board of Works", *The Daily News-Advertiser*, 13 January 1897.

No later than to-day I saw two does exposed for sale openly on Cordova Street. Is there no Game Protection Society to take the matter up? The sooner a few examples are made of these open infractions of the Game Laws the better, for if the present slaughter which spares neither age nor sex is kept up, the deer will soon be as rare as the buffalo.

Yours truly,
Venator

from *The Daily News-Advertiser*, 6 September 1891.

Left ca. 1895. Granville Street near 37th Avenue.

Top ca. 1895. Residence of Mayor Cope at 1100 Haro Street.

Bottom 1894. 33 Dufferin Street East (now 2nd Avenue East).

Top ca. 1898. The entrance to Stanley Park. Note the carbon arc lamp in the foreground and, to the left, the trestle and water main carrying water from the Capilano River.

Bottom ca. 1896. Beach Avenue west of Chilco Street, looking east.

It was after 1890 that we moved down to Beach Avenue.... You may remember how narrow and how crooked Beach Avenue was; not much wider than a buggy's width; a yoke of oxen abreast almost filled the whole of it; lined on both sides, either with bushes or greenery, or huge stumps, obscuring the sight; it was impossible to see down the trail more than a few yards.

I was in the garden. Suddenly I heard a man's voice exclaiming in alarm "Good God", and looking up, there were two men driving about eight oxen along the road, the earth was soft, and dusty, and their feet made no noise as they approached. Right beside, in the middle of the trail, my two little brothers, mere tots, were playing; another second or two and the approaching oxen would be on and over them. I grasped one, and pulled him inside the gate; then stepped out and grasped the other, and pulled him away too; how I did it in time I don't know. Great enormous beasts they were.

Mrs. Walter Frederick Evans, quoted in J.S. Matthews, *Early Vancouver*, volume 4, page 249.

It was a quiet Sunday morning in August, 1896. Mr. Hatch went down his garden somewhere about Fraser Street and 19th Ave., to feed his chickens. To his great indignation he found a huge black bear lying along a log deliberately breakfasting on one of his birds. He shooed it off into the bush that thickly covered the swampy ground towards Main St.

from William Fleming, "Memories of Early Vancouver", 1938, additional MS. 132, Vancouver City Archives.

My father was the first park keeper.... When Stanley Park was opened.... we went to live in the park lodge at the entrance.... Father laid out the first grounds, cut the first trails, did the first landscape gardening. Mother was actually, but father nominally, the first zoo keeper.... She had bears on chains for five years before they were put down in the old concrete bear pit.... I remember so well because a minister's wife poked the old bear, chained to the stump, with her umbrella, and the bear tore her umbrella and all or part of her skirt off.

Henry S. Avison, quoted in J.S. Matthews, *Early Vancouver*, volume 3, page 371.

Right 1897. By the Hollow Tree in Stanley Park. William Notman photograph.

9138—GREAT CEDAR TREE, STANLEY
NOTMAN
MONTREAL

STAFF. OF. LIFE.

I think it must have been in 1892 that we had the small pox scare in Vancouver. It was supposed to have come in by the "Empresses" from the Orient, for hardly anyone who had anything to do with the "Empress of China," "Empress of India," or "Empress of Japan," the C.P.R.'s first yacht-like liners, escaped it. It was a terrible July; yellow flags were everywhere....

It was the custom to put those stricken in an express wagon, and with the driver ringing a bell to keep people away ... the load of sick, frequently girls from Dupont Street, who had been visited by sailors from the "Empresses", would be driven down to the dock, and taken by boat to Deadman's Island....

Mrs. J.Z. Hall, quoted in J.S. Matthews, *Early Vancouver*, volume 1, number 114.

Carbolic acid, pure and simple, is an old and effective disinfectant, as is also chloride lime. You will do well to discourage the attention of any tramp smallpox germs that may be lurking around your back yard with a liberal dose of either of the above disinfectants. Atkins & Atkins keep a large supply on hand at Medical Hall, P.O. Block.

from *The Vancouver Daily World*, advertisement, 22 July 1892.

To get a proper idea of the extent of the innundations now spreading misery and loss throughout the Fraser River valley, one has to study the map of that part of the country. The immense acreage then found to be under water is appalling. The Pitt meadows, the plains in and about Harrison lake district, Matsqui prairie, part of Langley district, the greater part of Chilliwack, as well as all the islands in the upper part of the river are now under water.

...municipalities and the Government have lost heavily through the sweeping away of bridges and added to this is the tremendous loss of the Canadian Pacific railway and that of store-keepers in flooded villages.

from "The Fraser River Floods", *The Vancouver Daily World*, 6 June 1894.

Top left 1898. Telephone operators.

Bottom left 1892. Labour Day picture of Blake's Bakery staff.

ca. 1894. Chinese funeral on Westminster Avenue at Princess Street (now Main and Pender streets). C.S. Bailey and Co. photograph.

1898. Mule train for the Klondike in
front of Johnston and Kerfoot, 104-106
Cordova Street.

"I guess the Klondike gold rush really put Vancouver on its feet," Mr. Campbell said. "The city was teeming with people. There was a little rowdyism, but no real crime. Boats were being loaded with tons of supplies. Dogs were tied everywhere on the decks."

"Yes," Mrs. Campbell said, "even the children were training dogs in the streets during the gold-rush days. They had dogs of all kinds and they trained them to pull little wagons. Then they sold them to gold hunters going to the Klondike."

from "Some Real Rowdyism, But No Real Crime in The '90's", Police, Early Docket, 24 April 1940, Vancouver City Archives.

J.T. Luscombe, of 1216 Seymour Street, is a big, good-natured Englishman. He has no use for the Boers or in fact anyone that is "agin" the Mother Land. Yesterday, Mr. Luscombe, who is a butcher, turned up at the station to witness the departure of the soldiers. He drove down in his little cart, and it was just here where he made a great hit with the crowd. Attached to the side of the cart was a flag pole, from which floated the Union Jack. Tied artistically at the head of the pole was a large bunch of maple leaves, and dangling at the foot of the pole was a "boar's" head, through which ran a fierce-looking butcher knife. The affair caused great amusement among the crowd.

from *The Vancouver Daily World*, 24 October 1899.

There's a breath from Japan
　Of an ocean born air,
Like the blue water smell
　In an Argonaut's hair:
'Tis a carol of joy
　With a sweep wild and free:
And the mountains deploy
Round Vancouver Queen of the West,
　Where she sits by the seas,—
　By the Occident sea—
In her Orient vest,
　Babel Earth at Her Knee,
　And the heart of all nations
Alive in her breast.

from *The Daily News-Advertiser*, 7 November 1888.

Top 1889. Mount Pleasant looking north from 7th Avenue and Westminster Avenue, showing old False Creek Road and the bridge over False Creek on Westminster Avenue (now Main Street). H.T. Devine photograph.

Bottom 1898. Mount Pleasant nine years later looking north from vicinity of 9th Avenue and Quebec Street. S.J. Thompson photograph.

The Golden Years 1900–1914

"In 1910, Vancouver then, will have 100,000 men," declared boosters at the turn of the century: an ambitious slogan for a city of 27,000, but not a frivolous one. In the midst of the biggest boom it had ever seen, Vancouver reached its population goal of 100,000 in 1910 with a further jump to 115,000 by 1913, the year the boom collapsed. The golden years began in 1904, when eastern Canadian and western European capital spurred development of British Columbia's mineral, lumber and fishing resources. Vancouver, which had become the province's major transportation, trading and financial centre, plunged into land speculation and construction.

Streetcar lines spearheaded expansion beyond the two square miles where the population had been concentrated and opened up large tracts of land. By 1914 they provided access to Kitsilano, West Point Grey, Kerrisdale, Marpole, South Vancouver and Collingwood. Interurban lines extended to Lulu Island by 1902 and, later in the decade, as far as Abbotsford and Chilliwack. Single family houses went up everywhere. Working class people moved to small lots available in the east end: more prosperous citizens bought larger lots in the western suburbs. Factories and mills spread to the south side of False Creek, its position as the city's industrial hub consolidated by the creation of Granville Island in 1914. Schools, hospitals, sewer lines and bridges, including the Cambie and second Granville bridges, were constructed. Some of the city's finest landmarks date from this era: the Carnegie Library, the Post Office, the Dominion Trust Building — briefly the tallest in the British Empire — and its rival, the Sun-World Tower.

Above all, the city acquired a new tone, one considerably influenced by the influx of the British, who by 1912 represented over a third of the population. English visitors touring the city by bicycle, carriage or one of the city's rare automobiles were quite at home amid the clipped hollies, the parks and public beaches, the turreted Gothic houses of the West End and the mock Tudor mansions of exclusive Shaughnessy Heights.

Less at home were the growing numbers of Chinese, Japanese and East Indians who came to Vancouver during the decade. When, in 1907, a temporary recession interrupted the economic prosperity, local hostility towards these people intensified and an Asian Exclusion League emerged to decry their presence in the labour force. After anti-Oriental riots erupted downtown, the federal government tightened the already stringent restrictions against Asian immigration. But the problem would not go away. On 23 May 1914 the steamer *Komagata Maru* sailed into Vancouver harbour. Its East Indian passengers spent a stormy nine weeks in port trying to challenge the embargo on Asian immigration before finally departing in defeat on 23 July 1914.

The would-be immigrants could not have come at a more inauspicious time. Late in 1912 the boom in Vancouver had fallen victim to overexpansion and a depressed world market. By 1914 many businesses, from the Dominion Trust Company to suburban merchants, had suffered financial collapse and the city was full of unemployed. Adding to the gloom of this economic situation, the likelihood of war in Europe grew daily. Just twelve days after the departure of the *Komagata Maru* Canada entered the Great War.

Top ca. 1902. Dawson Hardware Co. Philip Timms photograph.

Bottom 1901. Shooting gallery on Cordova Street.

Page 48 ca. 1905. North side of Hastings Street, west of Hamilton Street. Philip Timms photograph.

It is not easy to look back on conditions of 100 years ago because there are so many matters which now enter into daily life as necessities that it is almost impossible to conceive of their absence. First, perhaps, of all is the railroad — but 25 years of the century had passed before there was a single mile of railroad in the world. To-day there are over 450,000 miles. Reverse, for a moment the wheels of progress and run back for a hundred years and what are the experiences. Many and many a mile stone of progress is passed before the journey has proceeded far. The telephone, phonograph and graphophone quickly disappear. Electric railways are lost and electric lights have gone out. The telegraph disappears. The sewing machine, reaper and thrasher have passed away, and so also have all India rubber goods. No longer are there photographs, lithographs, or cameras. The printing press dwindles rapidly in size until it becomes a clumsy hand machine. Planing and woodworking machinery go. There are no gas engines, no passenger elevators, no asphalt pavements, no steam fire-engines ... no celluloid articles, no wire fences, no time-locks for safes, no self-binders or harvesters... no cash registers or cash carriers, no great suspension bridges, no canals of any size, no magazine guns, no type-setting machines, no typewriters. All pasteurizing or knowledge of disease germs and microbes disappears. Sanitary plumbing is unknown and of antiseptics or anesthetics there are none. Water gas, soda water, air brakes, coal tar dyes, dynamos, steamships. Bessemer steel with its wonderful developments, dynamite, gun cotton, aluminum ware, ocean cables, enamelled iron ware, storage batteries, roller mills, knitting machines, tin can machines, artesian wells, lucifer matches, artificial limbs, nail machines, Xray apparatus, machines for woolen and cotton manufacture — all have disappeared.

from "The Wonderful Century", *The Vancouver Daily Province*, 15 December 1900.

Top 1900. City Hall on Main Street south of Hastings Street. The building was originally a market and later became a library after City Hall moved to Hastings Street. H.T. Devine photograph.

Bottom 1901. The *Empress of Japan* sails away through the First Narrows.

The Style That Stays

The smelts, oh, the smelts? We did not bother about them. The smelts were there in shiploads, yes, shiploads, you could fill a boat in fifteen minutes. As a girl, I have myself filled three or four sacks; potato sacks, and towed them behind the boat. You could almost tip a boat over, and fill it with smelts. But they have all gone now. Now, where do you suppose they went to?

Mrs. J.Z. Hall, quoted in J.S. Matthews, *Early Vancouver*, volume 1, number 22.

The big house, east side Carrall street, where we boarded, was over False Creek tide water. Household slops and garbage; oh, we just threw it out, and the tide took it away.

Mrs. Jos. W. Cameron, quoted in J.S. Matthews, *Early Vancouver*, volume 4, page 116.

At the period spoken of, concrete sidewalks were limited to the space in front of some of the more recently constructed down town buildings; all others, on Granville, Hastings, Cordova Streets were wooden planks running crosswise; in the residential streets all sidewalks were of wood, mostly five foot width crosswise save in the more sparsely settled, newer districts, where they were three planks lengthwise. The streets were largely macadam or wooden plank. In winter the macadam was muddy; the planks, frequently loose, had a nasty habit of squirting dirty water up the cracks between when a weight passed over, frequently soiling the trouser legs.

Major J.S. Matthews, quoted in J.S. Matthews, *Early Vancouver*, volume 1, number 107.

On the sunny slope which dips with gentle undulations into the golden west, and commands an exquisite panoramic eyeshot of the Gulf of Georgia, the mountains of Vancouver Island and Howe Sound, softly blue in the enchanted distance, the well-to-do of Vancouver have pitched their tents, and settled down amid surroundings the most salubrious and beautiful. Here they have transformed what was, ten years ago, a virgin forest, where the salmon berry, the salal, the huckleberry and the succulent skunk cabbage flourished in prodigal luxuriance in the fat and sappy soil, into a West End of which any city in all America might be proud.

from "The Stately Homes of Vancouver's West End", *The Vancouver Daily Province*, 10 November 1900.

Top Burnaby Street in the West End. Philip Timms photograph.

Bottom 1901. View of Coal Harbour and what is now North Vancouver from the roof of the Hotel Vancouver on the corner of Georgia and Howe streets.

1902. Parlour in the home of Claire
S. Downing at 1954 West Georgia Street.
Claire S. Downing photograph.

The "bar tender" or barman, was generally, a bright, strong, popular, and discreet man, and well dressed, and well paid. A big "schooner" of beer was five cents, and whiskey "two for a quarter" and help yourself. The original bottle was placed, on the bar, before you, and you and your friend poured into your glass what each wanted, the "bar keep" watched and filled the glass up with water, soda water, or ginger ale; that was all. To have measured it — as is done now — would have been a gross affront.

from J.S. Matthews, *Early Vancouver*.

On the Chinese New Year, for a week or so you could go down Dupont Street and you would see them, the Chinese, throwing fire-crackers and having all sorts of fun.... and if you'd look in a store they would hand you some Chinese candy or Chinese nuts or Chinese something. They were very generous that way.

from an interview with J. Rodger Burnes, number 175, Oral History Programme, Reynoldston Research and Studies.

...last Saturday night ... the Aldermen in company with several leading civic officials and a *Province* representative paid a visit to Shanghai alley, Canton street, Carrall street and Dupont street.

The party first visited Shanghai alley, which at the time was crowded with boys and young men gathered about the doors of the dens of vice which have recently been located there. A long string of red lights told all too plainly the nature of the resorts, but some of the denizens have gone still farther, and glittering name-signs were displayed. But as though this was not enough, from behind the curtains and through the half-opened doors the women of the street could plainly be seen inviting passers-by to enter. As quickly as visitors to the place left, the occupants of the room attired in the briefest of skirts, with the decollete apparel to the limit, took their choice from the waiting crowd about the door.

from "Officials Make Tour of Shanghai Alley", *The Vancouver Daily Province*, 19 November 1906.

Top Early 1900s. Production of *Trial by Jury* at the Vancouver Opera House, owned and operated by the CPR.

Bottom ca. 1900. Savoy Theatre at 133 Cordova Street.

Left 1905. Capilano Suspension Bridge across lower Capilano Canyon.

Top right August 1903. Picnickers on Second Beach in Stanley Park. Claire S. Downing photograph.

Centre right 1908. English Bay bathers with the old bathhouse in the background. Philip Timms photograph.

Bottom right ca. 1912. Self-appointed lifeguard, Joe Fortes, who taught many Vancouver children to swim. Stuart Thomson photograph.

When old Joe Fortes was first self-appointed
beach guard here at English Bay there was a
huge boulder at the foot of Denman street
— big as a house — and all women bathed to
the west of it and all men to the east.... But,
as time went on, women became bolder and
invaded the men's part, but still retained
their old style bathing suits ... with flounces
around the middle hanging like mudguards
on a motor car. It was a wonder they were
not drowned. They also wore stockings and
sandals; they looked very nice, too.

Then one day one impertinent hussy,
bolder than the others, went in bathing
without her stockings. She was a sight to
behold — she was bare naked right up to her
knees. The Women's Christian Temperance
Union wrote to the press about it and what
they wrote about the bold woman was
published in the newspapers. She sued the
W.C.T.U. for libel. The case went to court
and she got damages.

from Major J.S. Matthews, "The Great English Bay Scandal",
Early Vancouver, volume 7, page 154.

My country visit has left me badly tanned. I
would like to have it taken off before school
commences. Can you give me any assistance?

from "On Health and Beauty", *The Vancouver Daily Province*,
17 September 1904.

Mr. Mackay had one idea, which, had it been
carried out would have saved Vancouver
from the tragic lack of parks in the centre of
the city. He represented to the City Council
that they should acquire four or five large
squares of land between False Creek and
Burrard Inlet, to be used as parks, as
playgrounds for children, and places of rest
for the aged. He tried to explain to them
how the system of parks in the large cities of
Great Britain provides for this, and pointed
out that such parks would enhance the value
of the property surrounding them, and
urged that the acquisition of such open
spaces in the West End was particularly
desirable; but the only man who supported
him was David Oppenheimer; the others did
not see eye to eye with him, and a great
opportunity was lost.

A.P. Horne, quoted in J.S. Matthews, *Early Vancouver*, volume
4, page 346.

The operators and electric construction workers, embracing all the employees of the N.W. & B.I. Telephone company, with the bare exception of the office staff, went out on strike at 5 o'clock last evening. To-day Vancouver is practically without a telephone system with the exception of the long-distance lines, and the 1,000 instruments in this city are reduced from the position of useful conveniences of modern life to the comatose condition of the ordinary adornment of a plaster wall.... The immediate cause of the strike is the want of recognition of the union, according to the statement of officers of the latter.... According to their statement, their principal grievance outside of the question of low wages is that they do not get any allowances for sick leave.... If an operator is off duty for even half a day, she has to pay another girl to take her place in order to retain her situation.

from "Telephone Strike is Still Unsettled", *The Vancouver Daily Province*, 27 November 1902.

Now it was that the Asiatic Exclusion League was formed and, on Saturday night, September 9 [1907], a great rally of the league took place.... A monster parade marched down Hastings Street that night. First came the speakers and their lady sympathizers in horse-drawn carriages, followed by over 5,000 marching men, each with a white badge fluttering from his buttonhole.... Then someone shouted "on to Chinatown" and the trouble started.... On the first trip only rocks were thrown and hundreds of windows were broken. The second trip proved more vicious, for this time there was gunfire. When the mob grew tired of this they moved down to Japtown. Here they met stiff resistance but there was no shooting.... No Chinese or Japanese appeared on the streets for days. The Oriental sections of Vancouver were roped off by the police and remained under martial law for ten days.

from Albert Foote, "Vancouver Revolt Cost City $16,000", *The Vancouver Sun Magazine*, 6 September 1947.

Top left 1904. Chinese vendors on Dupont Street. Philip Timms photograph.

Bottom left 1906. Coal delivery wagons at the corner of Cambie and Robson streets.

1907. Nishimura Masuya's grocery at 130 Powell Street after the anti-Asiatic riots.

AN EDUCATIONAL INFLUENCE IN THE HOME
VICTOR VICTROLA
(Hornless Gram-o-phone)
Hear It To-day At The Nearest Victor-Berliner Dealers
Berliner Gram-o-phone Co., Limited, Montreal
When Thinking of Xmas Gifts REMEMBER THE VICTROLA

Gas Ranges

$1 DOWN AND $1 A WEEK buys a Gas Range.

The Burnside Gas Appliance Co.
1037-1039 Granville Street
Phone 3704.

Miss [Emily] Carr, who has just returned to Vancouver from Paris, where she spent a period of eighteen months in the study of art, and where she exhibited in the Salon, will be at home to her friends and to all in the modern French movement in art on Monday afternoon from 4 to 6 o'clock, and in the evening from 8 to 10, at 1465 Broadway west. The paintings which Miss Carr executed while abroad will be on view.

from "The Province's Page of Social and Personal News", *The Vancouver Daily Province*, 23 March 1912.

The smokers of Vancouver think they have won the greatest trick of all. It works out something like this:

A cigarette — sometimes it is a cigar — is only half used when its "puffer" boards a car. He then goes into the car and secures a seat close behind an open window, sticks his head out of the window and continues to smoke. The consequences are that most of the fumes from the weed float back into the car. The conductor is on the pay-as-you-enter platform and sees nothing. The passengers receive the full benefit.

We who suffer ask you gentlemen is it fair? Please abstain — or catch the next car.

from "Lady Van's Page", *B.C. Saturday Sunset*, 15 July 1911.

The dangerous nature of the tramway approaches to the False Creek bridge was illustrated last night when a runaway horse swerved into the car track and fell between the ties. The Fairview car, carrying homeward-bound theatre goers, was held up for nearly an hour while volunteers extricated the animal from its precarious situation.

from "Twenty Years Ago in Vancouver", *The Vancouver Daily Province*, 6 January 1921.

Not more than twenty-five cows shall be kept by any one person, family, partnership, company or corporation at any one time within the ... limits of the city.

from By-law number 263, 16 January 1902.

Hitherto in Vancouver, spinsters and widows with proper qualifications might vote at municipal elections but married women had no vote — though their husbands might qualify upon the wife's property.

Upon representation by the Local Branch of the National Council of Women of the manifest unfairness of these regulations, the City Council, in December 1910, unanimously passed a resolution favoring an amendment to the city charter, allowing married women the same voting privileges as men. This amendment to the charter was made at the last session of the legislature, and this year [1911] every woman (maid, wife, or widow), of the full age of twenty-one, who owns property in her own right within the city limits, and is entered on the voters list as the owner of this property, is qualified to vote at elections for Mayor and Aldermen, and for money by-laws.

from Mrs. C.R. Townley, "Married Women May Vote in the City of Vancouver", *Points in the Laws of British Columbia Regarding the Legal Status of Women*, 1911.

The first thing for which the fashions this year call is the natural figure. This means, in general, a waist that is not drawn in, and it is a matter for rejoicing that the fashionable clothes are designed for this fullness. No corset or waist should be drawn in about the waistline, particularly on young girls. The diaphragmic region is very tender and below this are many of the vital organs that do not have a bony protection as do the lungs. Pressure on this part of the anatomy easily reduces the actual size of the waist but at the expense of crowding these organs into the abdominal tract, where, with the old style of corsets, they are wholly unsupported.

But the natural waist corset is so long in the skirt, and so built that its greatest closeness and pressure are about the hips and along the line of the supporting abdominal muscles, which need this help in keeping the body in a natural position throughout the waking hours. These new corsets are large in the waist and very low in the bust to allow deep breathing from the diaphragm. This very act of proper breathing establishes a freedom of poise and is itself a source of good health.

from "In Fashion's Realm", *The Daily News-Advertiser*, 5 July 1914.

Duxbak

Waterproof Bias Velvet Brush Edge

Skirt Binding

is the best skirt binding ever produced, and it is waterproof.

It's made of a waterproof velvet, cut on the bias, attached to a brush edge. The top is finished ready to sew on, and does not require turning in. It cannot chafe the shoe, there being no braid surface on DUXBAK to cause friction.

DUXBAK is so durable your skirt will only need to be bound once, which means a big saving in time and money, to say nothing of the annoyance.

Take no other skirt binding but DUXBAK. It has the letters S.H. & M. on the back of every yard.

It's one of the S.H. & M. make.

The S·H·&·M· Co.

Manchester, Eng.
Toronto
New York

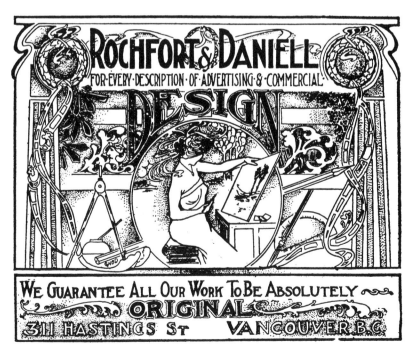

Oh, I will tell you a queer thing. I helped to beg for the first motor ambulance in Vancouver; it was hard work getting the money. And the first day it was taken out on a trial run, it ran over a man and killed him, in front of old Fader's grocery store; on Granville street; Pender and Granville, where the Bank of Montreal is now; he was the first passenger in our ambulance. It killed him outright; he was visiting here from the States. There was no organization; there was no I.O.D.E. or anything; we just begged, individually, for the ambulance; we were a sort of hospital auxiliary, but there was no president or anything.

Mrs. G.A. Bonnallie, quoted in J.S. Matthews, *Early Vancouver*, volume 6, page 97.

The Creche ... was established on April 3, 1912.... There is no thought of the Creche ever becoming self-sustaining as its only source of revenue is the nominal charge of ten cents a day assessed for the care of each child. Only children of working women are admitted and the maximum age limit is six years.

from Mayor James Findlay, "A Review of Civic Growth", *The Vancouver Annual*, 1912.

Let him [the average man] ask himself this: "Supposing I were a girl, good-looking, young and full of the joy of life, and I found that by working in a departmental store I could get only from $4 to $10 a week, and that by obliging my outwardly virtuous men friends from time to time I could make from $50 to $200 a week, which should I be likely to do?

Now that is exactly the question which confronts thousands of girls in Vancouver and elsewhere and those who have studied this question the closest know that the redlight districts of all large cities are largely recruited from the ranks of girls who cannot support themselves on the low wages paid to them by employers, who themselves are often members of Good Government Leagues or financial contributors to such institutions.

from J.W. Wilkinson, "Sex Prostitution Rampant — Who and What's to Blame", *The British Columbia Federationist*, 22 June 1912.

ca. 1910. Post Office on Hastings Street. Philip Timms photograph.

Top left 1908. Canadian Bank of Commerce on corner of Hastings and Granville streets. Canada Life Building adjacent. Richard Broadbridge photograph.

Bottom left 1913. Horse-drawn steam pumper going to a fire proceeds west on Georgia Street. St. Andrew's Church in background. Stuart Thomson photograph.

Top left 1912. Clearing Shaughnessy Heights with the help of a steam donkey engine, wire rope and gin pole. Richard Broadbridge photograph.

Bottom left ca. 1904. Arbutus from 5th Avenue looking towards Indian reserve and English Bay.

Top right 1911. Mrs. John Grimmett and her children on East 64th Avenue in the Municipality of South Vancouver.

Bottom right ca. 1910. Real estate agent's car stuck in the mud at 4th Avenue and Waterloo Road.

We looked at two sites across False Creek; one in Mt. Pleasant, one in Fairview ... that was in 1901....

At that time, of course, Mt. Pleasant and Fairview were leading residential districts. There were no such places as Kitsilano, Shaughnessy, Kerrisdale, Grandview, or Hastings as we know them today, and the West End was sparsely populated. There were locations in Mt. Pleasant which would have been suitable, but the Fairview site was more accessible on account of the bridges, and its position centrally to the density of population. Where, if you had a choice could you put a general hospital today, and improve upon the location? Then, again, remember, we had nothing to go on other than our idea of what a wilderness might grow into.

Mayor Thos. F. Neelands, quoted in J.S. Matthews, *Early Vancouver*, volume 5, page 149.

The throwing open for settlement of the first section of Shaughnessy Heights; reputed at the time to be the most wonderful residential section of Vancouver's future, unsettled all previous ideas of where a fine home should be built. The buggy was disappearing, the motor car was coming; distances were less formidable an obstacle than formerly. The verandah was still a necessity, but rapidly nearing its end, and soon to shrink into a mere porch. The broad verandah, the scene so long of evening parties, of Sunday afternoon gatherings, of sunshine and fresh air in the summer days was about to disappear. The Ford motor car killed it.

from J.S. Matthews, *Early Vancouver*, volume 1, number 104.

Talton Place was the first properly organized building project in the City of Vancouver; it was commenced in the spring of 1910.... The actual site [between 13th and 16th Avenues from Cypress Street to the Vancouver-Marpole Interurban Track] was chosen because of its commanding position, at a point high above the smoke of the city, overlooking English Bay; and at that time on the outskirts of the 'old' City of Vancouver. To the south and west there was practically no development at all; the land lay in clearing and in stumps; a few houses, to the north, scattered on the brow of the hill over-looking Kitsilano Beach.

Mr. McPherson, quoted in J.S. Matthews, *Early Vancouver*, volume 5, page 188.

ca. 1901. West Coast Indian women.
William Notman photograph.

No whiskey before whitemans. Whitemans come; he bring booze; spoil everything....

When Indians were dancing at potlatches, they danced by themselves; they did not hug a woman like the whitemans do. Hug woman no good. I never do it. Dance by myself. Only three Squamish mans now dance by themselves; nobody else.... Indian girls now paint faces like white womans, rouge lips, pluck eyebrows and make curve (arched eyebrows), put stuff on eyelids, high heels about four inches, long skirts down to ground; then they sweat and ... paint run all down face. Don't like. No good. No good hug womans. Indian paint not run off cheek like whitemans face paint.

August Jack Khahtsahlano, quoted in J.S. Matthews, *Early Vancouver*, volume 3, page 15A.

I hear you are asking for suggestions for occupations for women. May I say a few words on the crying need of the day in British Columbia? More than anything else, we want strong, capable women and girls who are willing to work in our homes. This we know is a problem common throughout the English-speaking world. British Columbia offers splendid wages, from $20 (£4) to $35 (£7) being paid per month. Our homes are planned to save work. Girls are well cared for, and have plenty of liberty. They are able each month to invest a little money in buying homes of their own and provide for their old age in case they do not marry. But, alas! this is the cry of most mothers and housewives. "Oh! I just get a really good, capable girl, then she gets married!"

I have lived in many parts of the world, but never have I seen better existing conditions for women and girls engaged in housework than are to be found in British Columbia. A good cook commands not only high wages, but respect; a good nurse is of the highest value, and a woman or girl who will do all kinds of housework is regarded in the light of a treasure. So British Columbia offers good homes, high wages, splendid climate, and good prospects for really good, useful women and girls.

I am, faithfully yours,

A LOVER OF BRITISH COLUMBIA

from *Women's Life and Work in British Columbia*, 27 May 1909.

Top 1913. Woman varnishing cans in a Steveston cannery. F. Dundas Todd photograph.

Bottom 1913. Indian family at ice cream wagon. F. Dundas Todd photograph.

Following page 1911. Parade celebrating the coronation of George V on Granville Street near Georgia Street. Stuart Thomson photograph.

C.M. Rolston then conceived the idea of the service station. Facing the street he built an open side shed — it was summer-time, 1908, of corrugated iron. It was about five feet deep, ten or twelve wide, and eight feet high in front, with plank floor. In the center was built a tapered concrete pillar, about three feet high, 12 inches square at top, and on this was placed a thirteen gallon kitchen water tank fitted with a glass (steam gauge glass) gauge marked off in one gallons with white paint dots. The tank was connected with the main storage tank. A bar room chair and a cushion for it completed the picture, excepting for the hose pipe, a piece, ten feet long, of garden hose without nozzle at end, which was drained with thumb and finger by the attendant after filling a car, and removed at night.

J.C. Rollston, quoted in J.S. Matthews, *Early Vancouver*, volume 2, number 309.

News reaches us from the Pacific Coast that another bread-making machine has made its appearance there which will displace thirty-two men and produce forty-four loaves a minute.... The unorganized bakery workers may draw their own deductions as to what will happen to them as soon as this machine is put into general use. Isolated and unprotected as they are today in their unorganized state, it will be hard for them to seek redress when their displacement begins. Organized and united with us, they would be in a position to protect themselves.

from "Bakers' Union Wrestling with Modern Problems", *The British Columbia Federationist*, 18 November 1911.

Mrs. MacKay's address: Public opinion allows woman certain fields of labor; but they are restricted fields. Her ability should test her in any department. She has a right to a voice in laws which control labor.... Every suffragette who throws a brick, every thoughtful one who writes, are helping the cause, for they must not stand still and repeat the mistake of the ancients. Already our civilization has developed the parasite — the woman who will take everything and give nothing. Everything bores her — her children bore her, and her husband who is a mere money-making machine.

from "Among Women's Clubs", *The Vancouver Daily World*, April 1912.

Top 1913. Crew inside Cedar Cottage sewer.

Bottom 1911. Hiring agency for loggers.

Left 1911. Building an extension to the Hudson's Bay Company's store at Georgia and Seymour streets with a steam shovel. Birks Building in background.

Top 1906. Sailing on the *Dorothy*. Claire S. Downing photograph.

Bottom ca. 1913. Bob Burman in the *Blitzen Benz*.

72

An illuminating address on the beautification of the city was delivered at the Canadian Club luncheon in Dominion Hall yesterday by Mr. Thomas H. Mawson, secretary of the British Institute of Art.... Mr. Mawson dwelt particularly with Stanley Park, which he said was regarded as Vancouver's most famous asset the world over. His principal scheme for improvement was that the mudflats of Coal Harbor near the park entrance should be converted into a great circular pond or lake with an encircling causeway or esplanade, and beyond should be a great natural museum of the fauna and flora of British Columbia.

"Coal Harbor at high tide covers an area of 51 acres. At low tide, or the greater part of the time it may be 10 acres. The rest is mud. What I want is a permanent sheet of water artistically treated and 35 acres in extent.... In the centre of this lake I want to see a great sculptured didactic monument. Round this monumental lake ... the people should be provided with a wide flagged path where they may perambulate free from the quick moving traffic....

from "Beautification of Coal Harbor", *The Daily News-Advertiser*, 28 March 1912.

The West Vancouver Ferry Company was formed about 25th Feb. 1910. Both boats were insufficiently powered, and when there was a good strong tide, had not the power to get in and out the Narrows, and used to lie in the shelter of Prospect Point awaiting a favorable opportunity.

Mr. J. Ollason, quoted in J.S. Matthews, *Early Vancouver*, volume 5, page 195.

Opponents of compulsory vaccination have made their protest in this city as they have elsewhere.... But as no good citizen would resist an order for the isolation of smallpox or diptheria in his own household, we may suppose that the whole protest is based on opposition to vaccination and disbelief in its merits.... Anti-vaccination societies and leagues have existed and argued for two generations. But they have not shaken the faith of the large majority that vaccination is the best known protection of a community from this awful pestilence.

from *The Daily News-Advertiser*, 11 February 1911.

The idea of an Exhibition within the reach of a five-cent carfare to the city's population gained ground, and in the year 1908 definite steps were taken to formulate plans for its consummation....

Hastings Park was chosen for the site of the Exhibition, despite initial opposition from racing men who, for some years, had operated a small racecourse there....

Sir Wilfred Laurier came to perform the opening ceremonies making the whole public awake to the great import of the occasion.

from "Infant Steps of Vancouver Exhibition", *The Vancouver Daily Province*, 2 September 1933.

There has been a little trouble in Vancouver over a Fourth of July celebration at the Dutch Grill. The orchestra played American music and did not wind up with "God Save the King", though the leader was asked to do so....

The conductor of the orchestra has explained that, not being British, it never occurred to him that to wind up in a British city should be the British National Anthem. The incident will seem trivial to some good people in the Old Land. But it is not. The Americans make a religion of their flag and the spectacular order of their patriotism. They will allow no other flag to be given a premier place in their communities no matter what the occasion; while, when they are abroad, they plant the Stars and Stripes on every proper and indelicate excuse....

The flag and the National Anthem are of like import. We do well to be even a little bit grouchy about them.

from "The British News of Canada", cited in *B.C. Saturday Sunset*, 5 August 1911.

Sea-Room! Sea-Room! Vancouver, child of the sea:
We have left the shore where the breakers roar,
and the rocks and shallows be:
We are steering straight with our human freight wherever the fates decree,
And many a town of old renown our harbinger shall be,
But there's never an one like thee,
Vancouver, child of the sea,
Never a city like thee!

from Sir Aubrey Neville St. John Mildmay, B.C. Provincial Archives, 1910.

Top 1912. Lacrosse game at Brockton Point between the New Westminster Salmonbellies and the Vancouver team.

Bottom 1911. Cougar hunt. Bullen and Lamb photograph.

On Sunday last a large number (several thousand) men gathered at Powell street grounds in response to a call for a public meeting issued by the committee having the unemployment matter in charge.... They were without arms. No threats, either against life or property, had been made. The speakers who were to address the gathering mostly belonged in Vancouver, some of them being officials of the Vancouver Trades and Labor Council and among the most widely known men in the labor movement in Canada.... No sooner was the meeting called that the law, in the shape of the city police, stepped in and converted a peaceable assembly of quiet and orderly men, women and children into a struggling mass of frightened humanity, fleeing for their lives from the brutal assault of the police acting under the Mayor's orders.

from "Cossack Rule", *The British Columbia Federationist*, 5 February 1912.

The Komagata Maru and her 352 Hindu passengers raised anchor and set sail a few minutes after 5 o'clock yesterday morning. The famous vessel and her human freight which have aroused the interest of the whole British Empire were in Burrard Inlet for exactly two months. The vessel arrived here on May 23 and departed on July 23. During the interim the most bitterly waged assault to which the Canadian immigration laws have been subjected was carried on and the victory rests with the latter.

In spite of many dire forebodings to the effect that the shipload of Hindus would finally succeed in securing admission to the Dominion and predictions that blood would be shed before the vessel again passed through the First Narrows, the Hindus left for home without a mark of violence and the immigration laws still stand supreme....

A large crowd of people remained on the waterfront to a late hour believing that force would have to be used finally before the visitors would consent to departure. As the hours wore on their numbers gradually diminished until at daybreak there were not more than 500 who had foregone the pleasure of a comfortable night's rest in order to witness the departure of the Komagata Maru.

from "Komagata is Homeward-Bound", *The Daily News-Advertiser*, 24 July 1914.

18 September 1912. Vancouver City Mounted Police posed under Lumberman's Arch at Pender and Hamilton streets on the occasion of HRH the Duke of Connaught's visit.

Right 1914. East Indians on the *Komagata Maru*. Leonard Frank photograph.

March 1916. Canadian battalion
entraining for overseas duty at the
Hastings Park railway siding. Stuart
Thomson photograph.

Answering the Call
1914–1918

Few cities in the British Empire were farther from the guns of World War I than Vancouver, yet few responded with as much patriotic fervour when the Empire entered the war on 4 August 1914. Thousands of men — many of them British born — departed for the front. At home, women spent hours knitting socks, and businessmen drilled with the home guard. Unfortunately, the war did not as quickly enlist the city's industries, and economic doldrums continued for another year. Construction lagged, although such remnants from the boom as the Georgia Street viaduct and the second Hotel Vancouver were completed, and the CNR arrived. During this period the city's population dropped by over 30,000, and would not return to the prewar level until 1919.

In the fall of 1915, Vancouver received its first major war contract, a $2 million order for munitions, and began a slow recovery. After the first shipbuilding contracts of 1916, the glut of labour became a shortage. Women, suddenly needed in the labour force, took over traditionally male jobs, becoming typists, stenographers, bank clerks, gas station attendants and munitions workers. Their participation in the war effort advanced the cause of suffrage and other rights that women had been demanding for years. In 1917, British Columbia's Women's Suffrage Act was passed, followed by the Equal Guardianship Act and in 1918 by the Minimum Wage Bill and the Mothers' Pension Act. Temperance preachers — and bootleggers — had their heyday too: the province's Prohibition Act passed on 20 December 1917 limiting alcohol purchases to two per cent "near beer," doctors' prescriptions, and exports.

Despite seeming prosperity, the work day still lasted nine or ten hours and wages lagged behind the soaring cost of living. Housing became expensive and scarce as construction was diverted to the war industries. Trade unions, strengthened by politically sophisticated British workers, began to agitate for better wages and working conditions. Boilermakers, sugar refinery employees, shipyard workers and civic employees all went on strike in 1917. A June walkout by B.C. Electric employees left public transportation to the company's competitors, open touring cars known as "jitneys." Although the streetcar employees eventually got their wage settlement, it was at the expense of the jitneys, which were abolished, and of the public, which had to pay a penny more for transportation. More labour unrest followed in 1918, including Canada's first general strike, a 24-hour "work holiday" in honour of a dead labour leader. Working days that year were further diminished by the fall's great influenza epidemic. By the time Armistice was declared on 11 November 1918, hundreds of local deaths had been added to the lists from the front. Even so, the news of peace brought a relieved population into the streets to join one of the greatest celebrations the city has ever seen.

Every home should be supplied
with the stirring music of the day

Music

Ye Olde Firme

stimulates

Patriotism

Victrola

Walter F. Evans, Ltd.

657 Granville Street

There was an awful lot of — you wouldn't call it romance — but excitement went with the First World War. The boys were all joining up, the boys that we went to school with. In 1914 the city wasn't that big you know and we all went down and saw the troop trains away and all this sort of thing. There was a lot of glamour because the boys were just going over for trips; you know, get a trip overseas and they'd be home in no time.

from an *Urban Reader* interview with Miss Dan Mitchell.

The dragnet for men of military age who have failed to register under the Military Service Act was spread by the military and police on Saturday and by 10 o'clock at night, after visits to rooming houses on Cordova and Powell during the morning and to the skating rink at night no fewer than 28 men of military age had been detained while later in the night, following visits to dance halls and other resorts, this number was further added to, although to what extent was not ascertainable late last night.

from *The Vancouver Daily Sun*, 18 November 1917.

This woman [Mrs. Duncan R. Reid] was a soldier's friend, and soldiers, like children — and dogs — have long memories for kind friends. She was of that legion to which all soldiers bend a grateful knee; akin to Florence Nightingale, only different; that great galaxy of devoted Canadian women, some rich, most poor, many unknown, who helped — in the Great War. She was a knitter of socks. Those there were may be who will smile — such plebian wear — but such as do are not soldiers, and smile without knowledge.

    With her own wrinkled fingers — she was about seventy then — this good friend knitted eight hundred single socks — four hundred pair — enough to outfit the battle strength of many a worn battalion; or one half sock for each day of the war.

Major J.S. Matthews, quoted in J.S. Matthews, *Early Vancouver*, volume 2, page 260.

ANSWERING THE CALL

Top 5 August 1914. *Vancouver Province* cartoon on the outbreak of World War I. "The whelps of the Lion are joining their sire."

Centre September 1915. Duke of Connaught, Canada's governor-general, inspects Women's Ambulance Corps at Hastings Park. Stuart Thomson photograph.

Bottom ca. 1917. One of the weekly shipments of "soldiers' comforts" in front of Mrs. J.Z. Hall's residence on Point Grey Road.

Top 1917. Women munitions workers at Vancouver Engineering Works Ltd.

Bottom ca. 1917. Launching a ship at J. Coughlan and Sons shipyard.

Claiming that they are not citizens of Canada and that they have not been enjoying "full rights as real citizens", that they have no hand or voice whatsoever in the legislation of this country, and emphasizing that "far from giving us the rights of the public life, we have been brutally deprived of the lawful and natural rights of humanity such as the entrance of dear wives and children who long to see us but are not permitted to land, while if we venture to go and see them we are afraid we should not be allowed to land again", a deputation appointed at a meeting on Sunday, representing the Hindus of Vancouver, yesterday waited upon Registrar R.S. Lennie to claim exemption from compulsory service.

from "Local Hindus Ask to be Exempted", *The Vancouver Daily Sun*, 13 November 1917.

During the war the Imperial Oil Service stations — they had three or perhaps four in operation then — were operated by young ladies; women of good family in most cases. They wore a uniform of khaki coat, breeches and leather leggings. They continued on this work until after 1919, when the troops returned. Their employment was a war emergency.

J.C. Rollston quoted in J.S. Matthews, *Early Vancouver*, volume 2, number 310.

The teamsters' union will, during the week, through a committee appointed at the last meeting, make a demand on the employers for a nine-hour day and time and a half for all overtime.

from "City in Brief", *The Vancouver Daily Sun*, 15 October 1917.

So marked has become the decrease in minor crimes and especially drunkenness since the advent of prohibition in the city that the need for an auxiliary jail has ceased to exist.... With prohibition in effect for less than two weeks now, the police court lists have been so radically curtailed that old members of the police force hardly know where they are at.

from "Enter Prohibition; Exit One Perfectly Good City Jail", *The Vancouver Daily Sun*, 12 October 1917.

In her address on food control, Mrs. Griffin [a member of the British Columbia advisory board to the food controller] showed the necessity of conservation and pointed out that although many people criticized the government for not first eliminating the profiteer and other forms of high financing, two wrongs do not make a right, and to continue on a plan of wasting the necessities of life because someone else is not pursuing an acceptable course would be very damaging to the nation as a whole.

from *The Vancouver Daily Sun*, 17 October 1917.

It is not enough to say that the normal consumption in Canada of wheat must be reduced by at least one-quarter and that of beef and bacon by one-third. The responsibility must be impressed upon every man, woman and child in the Dominion.... If you cannot fight you can at least help to feed the fighting men.... France has shed its life blood: will you not eat oatmeal or corn muffins one day in three or four instead of wheat breakfast-food or white rolls, in order to feed France?

from "The Food Problem and its Challenge", *The Vancouver Daily Sun*, 20 October 1917.

The city council at its special meeting yesterday afternoon, discussed the increasing number of automobile accidents, the advisability of framing some regulation requiring new drivers of cars to qualify for competency before being allowed to drive on business streets, and the damage done to pavements by heavy trucks, and finally appointed a special committee to enquire into the whole question.

from *The Vancouver Daily Sun*, 10 November 1917.

One of the most notable features of 1918 was the Minimum Wage Act, which provides that experienced women workers shall not be paid less than a living wage.

from Helen Gregory MacGill, *Laws for Women and Children in B.C.*, chapter 14, 1925.

Top 1916. The White Lunch.

Bottom 1916. Sawmill on False Creek. Granville Island is taking shape in the background.

Orders did not have much effect on juvenile Vancouver last night, for Hallowe'en was celebrated by the younger element with as much gusto as usual and the police department was given a busy evening. The requests that the youngsters behave themselves because of the great number of people lying ill in the city from influenza availed but little....

The usual masquerade balls of course were non-existent, since ten people, the largest number permitted to gather under the epidemic closing regulations, would not form the nucleus of a very hilarious dance. The orchestra, the hostess and about one guest would make up the whole crowd. Instead of public gatherings, the members of each family became their own entertainers and many of them enjoyed the best time they have had since influenza took up its temporary abode in Vancouver.

from "Police Kept Busy On Hallwe'en", *The Vancouver Sun*, 1 November 1918.

I was asleep when, at thirteen minutes to one, the blowing of factory and steamer whistles awoke me. I called Hughie, who jumped out of bed, and we opened the windows, and the glad tidings came in the easier. He looked out, and said that most of the houses around (Kitsilano) were lit up and that people were walking to town.

It is now ten minutes to 2 a.m., and there are still sounds of whistles blowing, and people shouting, and beating cans, but most of my neighbors must have gone back to bed because their homes are dark again. A few firecrackers and pistol shots are ringing out, and by the distant sounds I imagine the revelry in the city must be intense.

Major J.S. Matthews quoted in J.S. Matthews, "Germany Surrenders", *Early Vancouver*, volume 1, number 195.

It is not to be wondered at...that the returned veteran is, for a short period, restless and unable to find himself. It has taken months to make him a soldier and it will necessarily take time to make him a civilian again.

from *The Vancouver Daily Province*, 26 March 1918.

4 September 1918. A veteran of the battles of Vimy Ridge and the Somme, Flight Lieutenant Victor A. Bishop, crashed a plane into a West End house on Bute and Alberni streets, emerging unscathed.

Top left 1918. Crowd watches the "Human Fly", Harry Gardiner, climbing the Sun-World Tower.

Bottom left 11 November 1918. Returned soldiers parade on Granville Street near Hudson's Bay store to celebrate the end of World War I.

November 1927. Dave Spencer and
bathing girls in *The Attached Attaché*,
sponsored by the Kiwanis Club. Leonard
Frank photograph.

The Gilded Decade 1918–1929

Like every other community across Canada, Vancouver gave its returning soldiers a hero's welcome — but the welcome did not include jobs. Employment dropped while war industries such as shipbuilding faded away and a worldwide depression set in. By 1920 nearly 10,000 people in the city were jobless.

Although the days of full employment did not return, the postwar depression was over by 1922. Now that the Panama Canal, opened in 1914, made east coast and European markets accessible, Vancouver's ice-free harbour became a convenient shipping point for prairie wheat. In spite of prohibitive freight rates, grain exports went from 6,500,000 bushels in 1921 to 24,600,000 bushels in 1922 and continued to rise. On False Creek, warehouses, wharves, railway yards, processing plants and sawmills proliferated, spewing grime and soot onto surrounding districts. The Terminal City was now the leading commercial centre of Western Canada.

Rum-running became a lucrative business for Vancouverites after U.S. prohibition was declared in 1920. Rarely harassed by Canadian authorities, exporters sent liquor to America by ship, train, automobile and even back-pack. Local bootlegging had petered out after the 1921 Moderation Bill ended prohibition in British Columbia, but the drug trade prospered. Gossip circulated in the city about wild parties where gin shared the honours with cocaine. The 1924 murder of a servant girl in a wealthy Shaughnessy home and a cover-up of the investigation not only fostered such gossip, but confirmed the public's suspicions of corruption in high places.

The pace of life in Vancouver was accelerated by Ford and his fellow inventors. Gadgets like the vacuum cleaner freed more hours for leisure, but movies, jazz records and the radio quickly took up the slack. Downtown, automatic traffic signals were installed to regulate the growing flood of Model-Ts and McLaughlins. Car thefts became common and as early as 1919 criminal gangs were using automobiles to stage fast get-aways. By 1925 even the police had cars.

Physical development, however, lagged during the early '20s. University of British Columbia students, crammed for years into temporary buildings on the Vancouver General Hospital grounds, did not move to their new Point Grey campus until 1925. That same year the completion of the Second Narrows Bridge finally gave North and West Vancouver residents an alternative to the ferries. In 1926 a new building boom relieved the pressure created by thousands of newcomers arriving after the war. Rows of houses spread throughout the city and scores of commercial buildings appeared downtown. During the last year of the decade a new Hotel Vancouver and the Marine Building were started. Both were fine tributes to a year in which Vancouver broke virtually all its economic records and acquired 79,000 people and 25 square miles through amalgamation with South Vancouver and Point Grey. Unfortunately, the good times did not last.

Sunday, as things are, is a day of incredible dullness in British Columbia. Youths and girls deprived even of the healthy and innocent pleasure of a game of tennis, lounge about the streets and get into mischief. The damage done to seats in parks and at the beaches bears witness to the effects of the fatuous and narrow-minded restrictions from which the young and vigorous portions of the population suffers. Fortunately bathing is not yet a prohibited sport; though why it should be lawful to play and exercise in the water and not on the land passes the wit of anyone but an official of the Lord's Day Alliance to discover.

from "Sundays", *The Western Idea*, 30 July 1920.

No, the veterans were not treated very well in the First War. And that's why the Legion and other organizations put up such a fight.... The First World War men knew that they hadn't had a fair deal, and they were fighting for the younger ones.... Somebody started a rumour that all veterans were drunkards or something like that. I don't know what it was; just it was darn hard to get a job if you were a veteran.

from an interview with Mr. Thomas Cecil Scott, number 46, Oral History Programme, Reynoldston Research and Studies.

The present situation has been carefully analyzed by impartial students and observers and the only conclusion they can come to is that an effort is now being made to OVERTHROW our present CONSTITUTIONAL GOVERNMENT; TURN DOWN THE BRITISH EMPIRE; TEAR DOWN THE FLAG and establish in the place thereof A BOLSHEVIKI form of government.

And the STRIKE LEADERS ADMIT IT.... The RETURNED SOLDIERS ARE NOT OPPOSED to unions and constitutional means of improving the worker's position, but we are most emphatically opposed to revolution, and that is what this massed strike amounts to.

from "This Is Not a Strike But a Revolution", *The Vancouver Daily Worker*, 14 June 1919.

Top 1922. House at 3689 Selkirk Street in Shaughnessy Heights. Leonard Frank photograph.

Bottom 1923. Laying the cornerstone of the Science Building at the University of British Columbia. Students began classes at the new Point Grey campus in September 1925.

Left 1920s. Constable Duncan McTavish at Abbott and Hastings streets with portable traffic signals. Stuart Thomson photograph.

Top 1919. Log bridge over the Seymour River in North Vancouver. Leonard Frank photograph.

Bottom 1924. Hastings Park auto camp. Stuart Thomson photograph.

Right 1924. Three-legged race at Crescent Beach during Henry Birks and Sons company picnic. Stuart Thomson photograph.

But no province or state on this continent has a richer mountain heritage than our own British Columbia, and yet we ourselves know so little about it and value it at so low a price....

A boat journey of less than four hours from Vancouver to the head of Howe Sound (a delightful outing in itself) brings the traveller to Squamish, from which can be seen the glistening peaks of the Garibaldi district. Then a short rail journey on the Pacific Great Eastern twenty miles only, passing by the deep gorge of the Cheakemous River, and we are ready for a tramp up Stoney Creek. By nightfall we camp on the Black Tusk Meadows, five thousand feet above sea-level.

[Early in 1921 Garibaldi Park was created by the Provincial government.]

from Rev. A.H. Sovereign, "Glorious Garibaldi: The Canadian Playground in British Columbia", *The British Columbia Monthly*, October 1919.

Prevention of the pollution of the bathing beaches on English Bay is one of the most important health problems facing the city at the present time, according to A.D. Creer, C.E., at one time engineer in charge of the Greater Vancouver sewerage system.... The speaker pointed out that three large sewers now emptied into False Creek and two others into the waters on the south bank of the bay. No serious pollution had occurred as yet, but with the increasing population of the city it would become a real danger, and the problem of caring for this drainage should be considered at once.

from "Prevention of Pollution of Beaches Urged", *The Vancouver Daily World*, 28 February 1924.

At this period of the season, it is quite easy to distinguish the carefully groomed, from the carelessly groomed women. Sun and mosquito favor no one in particular — and both those powers that be, leave behind them footprints on the sands of — complexion. The wise woman does not allow any footprints to take root, by a lavish use of face cream.

from *The Western Idea*, 13 August 1920.

CRYSTAL POOL
BEACH AVE. at NICOLA ST.

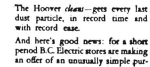
No question about I paid protection in Vancouver for years when I was on Granville Street bootlegging.... Pay directly to the dry-squad man, one man at a time. Two men would come up to your place once a month. In theory they were up to search the place, but they weren't searching ... and one would walk away from the other, and you knew which one your contact man was when he would walk into a room by himself. You followed him in, gave him the $25 and he'd put it in his pocket and turned around and said to his partner: "Well I guess there's nothing here. Let's go."

from an interview with Sheldon Rogers, number 91, Oral History Programme, Reynoldston Research and Studies.

Christian burial was accorded a few days ago in Vancouver to the drug-ravaged remains of a once beautiful woman whose life and death constitute a mute appeal for pity and a tremendous indictment of the drug traffic.

The circumstances surrounding the death and burial of Paula McCabe, former wife of a United States senator, and one of the best known denizens of Vancouver's underworld, are unfortunately similar to those which surround the end of many other addicts....

Time and again she tried with the help of others, to give up the terrible habit which had made her a woman of the streets, but after each attempt she succumbed to the temptation....

Several times during her periods of partial recovery ... she attended meetings of those who were endeavoring to aid her and those in similar plight and exhibited her arms and legs to show the innumerable marks which the needle had left upon her, in order that these girls might realize the havoc which the habit had wrought.

from Noel Robinson, "Underworld Leader Once Social Belle Dies Drug Victim", *The Vancouver Daily Star*, 8 May 1921.

The great World War, by crowding the gates of death, gave a mighty impetus to Spiritism.... The charlatan's statement of the possibility of speaking with ... loved ones who had been suddenly called from life was too subtle and too powerful for [people] to resist.

from "The Dangers of Spiritism", *The Bulletin*, 28 August 1925.

Fate of Vancouver's walkathons will be decided at a special meeting of the City Council Thursday.... Possibility of mental abnormalities developing in contestants, either during the contest or later in life, as the result of participation in the "walkies", was forecast by the health officer. He added that this might "accelerate the increasing demand upon our asylums for the insane...."

"Eighteen hours a day on foot is too long for youth," Dr. McIntosh reported.

from "Says Walkies Menace Sanity", [c. 1927-31], additional MS. 97, Vancouver City Archives.

Vancouver women had at last succumbed to the craze for bobbed hair. Men commented that it was the first time they had ever seen women's ears on the street.

from "Twenty Years Ago", *The Vancouver Sun*, 5 September 1946.

The practice of courting in automobiles in Vancouver has got to cease or it will land the offenders in court. The city fathers have been looking into the matter, it is believed at the instigation of the city mothers! Inspector Hood, who is the moving spirit in the crusade, describes the habit as "dangerous". He has already been nicknamed "Inspector Hoodoo" by one gay Lothario who says he can drive more safely in a compromising attitude. "More waist, less speed," he says in effect.

from *The Western Idea*, 9 July 1920.

A policy of strict silence is being carried out by those connected with the investigation into the death of Janet K. Smith, a Scotch nursemaid who was found shot in the Osler avenue home, where she was employed, last summer....

A story to the effect that after a wild party at a certain Shaughnessy Heights home a number of local men visited the Baker house and that on Miss Smith exhorting them to be quiet she was chased upstairs to the bathroom, where she fell and struck her head against the bath and was killed, a shot being later fired into her brain to give the impression of suicide or accidental death, has also been proved a canard as have a number of other sensational theories....

from "Mystery Probe is Futile", unidentified newspaper clipping, 26 January 1925.

The rising generation, with immature thoughts and unformed minds ever ready to be subtly worked upon, is being brought directly under the influence of the American silver-sheet. Who can tell what the result may be...?

But of vastly more importance than the problematical question of Americanizing Canada is the influence, mental and moral, which the plays exhibited are having upon our children. The motion-picture theatre is the cheapest and handiest form of entertainment that we have, and it has an enormous fascination for the youngsters....

When the lady in the picture leaves her husband, in a high temper, for her country home the picture then shows the interior of her drawing room and discloses to our view a man, in the act of kissing her, it comes with somewhat of a shock to hear the sweet little girl of eight exclaiming triumphantly, "I knew she would have a man with her." It may probably mean nothing to the child, yet, on the other hand, her head is becoming filled with the sordid things of life — and who knows what form her thoughts may take?

from Emily Wright, "Motion Pictures and their Influence upon Children", *The British Columbia Monthly*, March 1920.

Another abortive effort in favour of Sunday concerts was made Wednesday at the meeting of the finance committee of the city council. A delegation of women from the British Progressive League, headed by Mrs. Morewood Clark .... pointed out that Alderman Almond delivered ice cream of a Sunday, and Ald. Worthington sold drugs and sundries. She thought if it was all right to do the one it was all right to listen to music on Sunday.

There was a general expression from the aldermen that if one theatre was granted the privilege of Sunday concerts ... this would be the thin edge of a wedge for open theatres on Sunday, with pictures and everything.

from "Women's Organization Fails in Plea for Sunday Concerts", *The Vancouver Daily World*, 7 February 1924.

All drivers of automobiles must remain standing whilst a funeral procession is passing.

Speed limits — 25 miles per hour in open country; 15 miles per hour through cities, towns, villages and wooded country.

from The B.C. Motor Act, 1925.

1925. Dainty Dates Company exhibit at the Vancouver Exhibition in Hastings Park. Stuart Thomson photograph.

I remember one time in the early days of Vancouver when we used to ride on the left side of the road.... Nineteen twenty-two they changed over.... I remember that Sunday quite well. I went out into the street to watch it happen and everybody drove so carefully, suddenly changing to the other side of the street; there were no accidents at all. One thing it did upset. A corner drugstore used to be a street car stop would suddenly find itself on the wrong side of the street when they changed the traffic. It upset a lot of shop keepers at various strategic corners that were no longer where the public got on and off.

from library workshop, interview number 179, Oral History Programme, Reynoldston Research and Studies.

United States customs officers seized two car loads of shingles at Sumas, Wash. Wednesday night, when the cars were found to contain 72 sacks of liquor, valued $5000. Suspicion was aroused when the officers noticed mud and grass on the shingles while they were inspecting the freight train. This led them to believe the shingles had been unloaded, then put back in the car, somewhere outside a shingle mill. One car, consigned from New Westminster to Utica, Ill., had 58 sacks concealed under the shingles.

from *The Vancouver Sun*, 22 September 1927.

The latest explanation of the failure of salmon runs in the Fraser river, Vancouver, during the last few years comes from a coastal Indian who believes that the salmon have been offended by the prevalence of jazz music.

The women of the tribe, whose duty it is to play soothing melodies from the banks of the river, have forgotten the old-time favorites of the salmon and are resorting to the modern syncopated melodies.

from *The Vancouver Sun*, 22 October 1927.

Top 1928. New Westminster Fair ice cream stand. Leonard Frank photograph.

Centre 1924. CNR Radio Car.

Bottom 3 August 1921. Hudson's Bay Company picnic on the Union steamship *Cheam*.

Top 1928. Blackburn's Service Station and Used Car Lot at Robson and Seymour streets.

Bottom 23 August 1925. Delivery trucks on Water Street.

[Vancouver's Chinatown] has, of late years, spread amazingly. Residential localities which, until lately, were occupied by people who were white, at least, are now entirely Chinese. Business blocks, which a few years ago were occupied by Canadian firms are now filled with the goods of the Oriental. It may be said that this is part of the price of the war but, if so, it is surely none the less deplorable. Canadian business men and Canadian householders did not take up arms that their businesses and their homes might be taken over by Chinese. That the Chinese were our allies does not seem to the soldier citizen a satisfactory reply to this. And though as yet this new Chinatown has not all the objectionable features of the old Pender street district, the Chinaman quickly stamps his characteristics on any building he occupies, and this district is already sufficiently Chinese.

from "Cleaning Vancouver's Chinatown", *The British Columbia Monthly*, February 1921.

Nova Scotia and B.C., during the fruit canning and packing and fish run seasons rescind the restrictions of their Factories Act as to age, hours, commencement and cessation of work. The latter Province entirely and wholeheartedly states that the prohibitions as to all children, young girls and women are not binding upon employers during these seasons.

from Helen Gregory MacGill, "The Child in Industry", reprinted from *Hospital Social Service*, volume 13, 1926.

It would appear from our observations that the policy of the City Hall is to employ girls only for stenographic work and such work as the operation of the addressograph machines. In this matter the policy appears to differ from that of the majority of commercial concerns.

The employment of girls for certain work would effect economies in salaries and superannuation, as the salaries paid to them would be more in accordance with the value of the work done.

from report of Helliwell, Maclachlan & Co., "Survey of Accounting Methods", to Mayor Malkin, 16 October 1929.

5 January 1928. Japantown. Powell Street east of Main Street.

"Be it ever so humble. There's no place like home."

THE GREAT WORK OF LIFE INSURANCE IS THE PRESERVATION OF THE HOME —

LIFE INSURANCE SERVICE

Overnight, almost it has been recognized that the Panama Canal makes Vancouver the port of Western Canada, the Montreal of the Pacific coast, with a vaster potential trade than Montreal ever knew rapidly developing. The word has gone abroad all over the continent: "Watch Vancouver, B.C."

from "Time to Extend City Limits to Accommodate People Soon to Crowd in", *The Vancouver Daily World*, 12 February 1924.

One of the most familiar waterfront sights in Victoria or Vancouver is the numerous lumber mills, with their belching smokestacks and clouds of steam from coughing exhaust pipes. Add to this the constant scream of saws, the rumble of machinery, punctuated by heavy thumps of the huge logs as they are turned this way and that way by the powerful steam-niggers as though they were no more than match stalks, the large ocean-going steamers loading lumber at the wharves, the huge booms of logs being rafted into position, tug boats scurrying hither and thither, and you have a picture of commercial activity that once seen is never forgotten.

from "British Columbia's Major Industry Reaps Big Harvest", *The B.C. Electric Employees' Magazine*, November 1928.

Old Age Pensions were the most outstanding legislation in the session of 1927. Here again British Columbia led in social advance. Urged by the Government of British Columbia, the Dominion Government passed an Act desired by this Province to enable them to give aid and succour to our old people.

from Helen Gregory MacGill, "Laws for Women and Children in British Columbia", 1928.

Vancouver will have no skyscrapers if the City Council accepts the advice of its Town Planning Commission. Answering an enquiry ... this morning, the commission again endorsed the provision of the city charter which requires all buildings to be within ten storeys in height or 120 feet.

from "Would Prohibit All Skyscrapers Here", *The Vancouver Daily Province*, 25 October 1929.

Top 1928. Granville Street looking north from Pender Street. Leonard Frank photograph.

Bottom 1928. Looking north on Howe Street. Second Hotel Vancouver and the Vancouver Block building in background.

Right 1927. Granville Street near Robson Street, looking north. Second Hotel Vancouver on the left.

Percy Williams, a Vancouver-born boy, earned the soubriquet of the "world's fastest human" at the recent Olympiad at Amsterdam, when he won the 100 metres on August 1 from the greatest galaxy of sprinters from other countries ever assembled together at one meet.

from C.R. Foster, "Greater Vancouver Leads Canada in Variety of Sports", *The Vancouver Daily Province*, 31 January 1929.

Entertaining at "Hycroft," the palatial home of General and Mrs. A.D. McRae, is always most lavish, but possibly no party of the many to which smart society has been bidden in the past years, could quite equal the brilliance of atmosphere that prevailed at the Spanish costume party held New Year's Eve.

The ballroom had been transformed to represent a Spanish court of the eighteenth century and both Mrs. McRae and the General chose costumes to depict the leading characters in the very popular Spanish play, "La Duenna,"....

The guests, however, did not confine themselves, in the matter of costumes, to ladies and gentlemen of the court or to any special period, but in a gay riot of color appeared as senors and senoritas, matadors, toreadors or Spanish dancing girls, with the odd carefree Don Quixote.

from "Hycroft Setting for Gay Spanish Party", *The Vancouver Sun*, 2 January 1929.

"The market which could not come down" broke into a frenzied panic at this morning's opening in Wall Street, following a steady accelerating slump of weeks which had gathered alarming momentum in the last few days. Nothing less than the outbreak of another war could have so set the continent by the ears and word came that the European exchanges had broken, making the debacle a world-wide affair.

Men hurried along the streets in the cities of Canada and the U.S. faces pale and lips quivering; little knots formed in offices, with working discipline gone as often garbled versions of the break, which could hardly be exaggerated, flew around.

from "Toronto Market in Panic Today", *The Vancouver Daily Province*, 29 October 1929.

Top 1926. Worker "corking" (caulking) pipe at the Vancouver Engineering Works.

Bottom 1920s. Salesmen at Kelly Douglas, wholesale grocers.

Left 1920s. Escape artist Harry Houdini performing outside the *Sun* newspaper office on West Pender Street. W.J. Moore photograph.

1938. Single unemployed men on the
march, Hastings Street east of Main
Street.

The Hungry Thirties
1929–1939

In the fall of 1929 the Wall Street stock market began to decline and then, in late October, broke in the two heaviest days of trading ever recorded. Vancouver papers reported the losses, but failed to predict the chain reaction of economic catastrophe and ran headlines such as "Recovery From Market Crash May Take A Year." In December 1929 Vancouver voters optimistically endorsed by-laws to finance the Sea Island Airport, Burrard Street Bridge, and other public works.

But the city was economically dependent on the export of lumber, salmon, minerals and wheat, and vulnerable. When the bottom fell out of these markets the number of jobless soared. As early as January 1930 the unemployed gathered on the Powell Street grounds to demand a federal unemployment insurance scheme and organize forays to beg for food. By the winter of 1932-33, fifteen per cent of the city's population, nearly 40,000 people, required some form of public assistance.

The new airport opened in 1931 and the Burrard Street Bridge in 1932, but other projects were crippled by the lack of funds. An unfinished Hotel Vancouver at Georgia and Burrard brooded over the downtown through most of the Depression. The old Second Narrows Bridge, damaged in a shipping accident in 1930, rusted in the rain, unrepaired and closed to all traffic until June 1934.

As jobs disappeared, families who failed to pay mortgages or taxes were evicted from their homes. Teachers were only one group of workers who took pay cuts in order to keep their jobs. Single women, deeply resented by men if they tried to compete for jobs, had a difficult time getting either work or relief. Hundreds of unemployed single men rode the freights to Vancouver where winter was milder than in Moose Jaw or Kenora. At first they settled in hobo "jungles," but city officials, fearing outbreaks of typhoid or Communist agitation, burned the "jungles" and sent many of the men to relief camps in B.C.'s interior. Deserting the camps each spring, men concentrated in Vancouver to protest their 20 cent-a-day wage and spartan living conditions. Clashes were frequent between demonstrators and police, but the most notorious came in 1935, when Mayor McGeer read the Riot Act to a group of unemployed demanding relief or jobs, and in 1938, when the Post Office and Art Gallery were occupied.

In the early years of the Depression the wealthy took advantage of depressed real estate values to buy property at tax sales. For those with money, elegance was never so cheap: domestic help could be had for $10 a month, and dresses and prime beef were inexpensive. The papers were filled with descriptions of gala events. For those less fortunate, entertainment was the only escape, and people flocked to movies and dance halls, or spent their free time by the radio.

By 1936, there was evidence of a slow recovery. Large crowds joined in the city's 50th Jubilee celebrations that year, and a new city hall, the most ambitious of the work projects, was completed. The Lion's Gate Bridge was ready for traffic in 1938 and the Hotel Vancouver finally opened the following year. But for most people the Depression dragged on until the biggest public works project of all: World War II.

Top 1931. Looking south on Burrard Street towards the skeleton of the new Hotel Vancouver. Leonard Frank photograph.

Bottom 7 April 1930. Boundary Road with North Burnaby on the right, East Vancouver on the left. W.J. Moore photograph.

We looked down at everything — even the Marine Building had dwarfed during our climb [of the new Hotel Vancouver]. The city was despondently dirty beneath the murky haze that hung like a blanket of soot-stained steam; distantly clanging street cars crawled moodily along grey Granville street; even the greenery of the Park looked sorrowful through the haze....

Yet there was something that attracted. Was it the familiarity of home? Or was it the spirit of progress that rose from it like heat waves — the unmistakable yet indefinable thought that here was a city with — with growing pains.

from "Sport of Building Climbing", *The Vancouver Sunday Province*, 17 May 1931.

Two or three minutes and the new airport was on our left, a bleak, flat, dirty expanse of mud, broken by patches of disgusted-looking grass doing its best to soften the uninviting landscape then, a glance at the ripe-orange administration building, nearly completed, and the two candy-stick hangars with their red-and-white stripes, transformed the drearily-hopeless scene into one of bright optimism and a promising future.

from "Afternoon Auto Ambles About Vancouver", *The Vancouver Sunday Province*, 18 January 1931.

Frank Gilbert, who owns one of the Aeronca planes at the Sea Island airport vouches for this one. Recently ... he brought his plane down in a field near Chilliwack and went into the city. On his return he found some of the contented cows calmly munching the fabric of the fuselage. He managed to borrow a sheet and make temporary repairs to fly back to Vancouver.

from "Valley Cows Make Hearty Meal Off Plane Fuselage", *The Vancouver News-Herald*, 9 May 1933.

"They would!" is a common expression these days, and it was probably uttered by several thousand persons the other night when the Granville street bridge opened about 5:15 o'clock.... The dislocation of business and individual inconvenience of opening a draw bridge in the rush hours cannot be overestimated.

from "Bridge Open", *The Buzzer*, 16 October 1931.

August 1931. Southeast corner of Hastings and Columbia streets.

Top 1930's. Mothers' Council march for the unemployed.

Bottom 1931. Distribution of food to the unemployed in a "jungle" at the east end of False Creek. The man on the right in the striped suit is Rev. Andrew Roddan. W.J. Moore photograph.

I visited the 'Jungle' below Georgia viaduct.... There are about 250 men there. Grounds are filthy and covered with decaying garbage, with open toilets. Flies swarm over everything and on all open food. I consider that, with the rainy season approaching, we are in grave danger of an epidemic of typhoid or other disease. Many of the men are lying on the ground which is becoming damp, and they are certain to suffer from bronchial and rheumatic troubles.

from "Fear Typhoid From Jungles", *The Vancouver Sun*, 4 September 1931.

Have you a little garbage to dispose of today? If you have, and if it is breakfast, luncheon or dinner table garbage, and if you happen to live in the West End or downtown, please do not thoughtlessly toss it into the garbage can.... But place it carefully on the ledge of the backyard fence.... For, if it is carefully disposed along the top of the fence, out of reach of greedy dogs, the two-legged scavengers who inhabit the jungles of our fair city will be along, before dawn, to pick it up and fill their empty stomachs with it.

from James Dyer, "Any Garbage Today?" *The Vancouver News-Herald*, 3 December 1934.

Vancouver offers the greatest inducement to the family working-man...the cost of living there being the lowest among eight of the chief cities of Canada for which complete data is available. For slightly less than $15 a week the working-man with a family of five can pay rent for a six-roomed house with modern conveniences, fuel and food bills....

from "Living Cost Cheapest Here", 30 May 1933, *Unemployment and Relief, City of Vancouver*, volume 8, number 2, Vancouver City Archives.

There are store clerks employed in this city for the coolie wage of five dollars per week.... There are young girls employed throughout the city, earning from two to five dollars per week for eight hours per day.... I have...come to the conclusion that the Minimum Wage Act is but a fairy tale, and that those who are supposed to enforce it should be ashamed to take the money which the harassed citizens pay them.

from V.W.F., "Wages and Hours", *Vancouver Through the Eyes of a Hobo*, 1934.

Third eviction of relief families living in furnished quarters will take place Monday, when approximately 300 tenants will be removed from their homes, declares President L. Smith of the Lodging and Restaurant Keepers Association.

The rooming-house operators, seeking a higher shelter rate, have twice made general evictions involving about 150 families. The city-made temporary shelter payments and will likely do so again Monday.

from "More Evictions Planned Monday", 1 April 1933, *Unemployment and Relief, City of Vancouver*, volume 8, number 2, Vancouver City Archives.

The security of employment and fear of future misery nurtured by steadily decreasing earnings, strongly affects the atmosphere of homes. Where the head of the family has an assured job entitling him to a pension, or where he already has benefits by a pension, the tension is removed, and the child of that family is shown to be less nervously strained than that of the neighbor's who, no worse off, has the fear of tomorrow pressing on the peace of today.... One teacher reported that the children would do anything rather than confess that their parents were unemployed.

from "Unemployment Claimed Bad for Child's Mind", *The Vancouver News-Herald*, 24 April 1933.

In a vigorous and inspiring address, Percy Bengough, vice-president of the Trades and Labor Congress of Canada, emphasized ...that the effects of the depression should be fought actively rather than suffered passively.... "Unemployment today has reached such a stage in length and intensity," he said, "that it is the cause, rather than the effect of the depression...."

from "Retrenchment Plan is Insane Policy", *The Vancouver News-Herald*, 15 January 1934.

Tear gas and police clubs broke up a demonstration of longshoremen and their sympathizers, nearly 1,000 in all, who marched on Ballantyne Pier shortly after 1 o'clock this afternoon.... The marchers approached Ballantyne Pier along Heatley avenue carrying a Union Jack at their head. Some of them wore medals.

from "Scatter Along Railway Track", 18 June 1935, Strikes Docket, Vancouver City Archives.

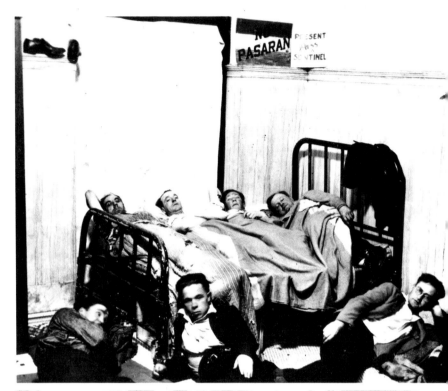

Top 1938. Unemployed. The poster on the wall "No Pasaran" (They shall not pass) is an anti-Fascist slogan from the Spanish Civil War.

Bottom 1930s. Chinese in front of a cleaner's store in Chinatown.

To dial any figure, place your finger firmly in the hole in the dial through which the figure is seen. Pull the dial around to the right until your finger strikes the finger stop. Then remove your finger and let the dial return to normal position without touching it.

from "How to Dial", *City Hall Telephone Directory*, 1930.

Do not think of baths in terms of cleanliness alone. Instead view the convenient hot and cold water faucets and the gleaming tub in your bathroom...as equipment as useful to you in keeping pace with this strenuous life as your alarm clock or coffee percolator; the twenty-four hour supply of hot water from your automatic gas water heater as necessary as the comfortable bed in which you sleep.

from "The Secret of Loveliness is the Bath", *Home Service News*, April 1932.

"Well, I move," said Ald. H.J. DeGraves, "that we do not proceed with any more baiting. We can spend our money to feed unemployed instead of feeding earwigs...." Ald. R.N. Fraser, however, objected. He said he had numerous complaints from people in West Pt. Grey about earwigs, and he thought they should have the benefit of the service if they desire it.

from "To Discontinue Earwig Baiting", 25 February 1932, *Unemployment and Relief, City of Vancouver*, volume 8, number 1, Vancouver City Archives.

Woman is responsible for the millions of men walking the streets. Half the depression can be traced to the same cause....

If every woman who has a male member in her family was compelled to give up her job, TWO-THIRDS OF CANADA'S UNEMPLOYED MANHOOD WOULD GO BACK TO WORK! They in turn, would take care of the women by marriage. Homes would be built; furniture bought; automobiles, radios, electrical appliances, and hundreds of other items would be purchased. Trade would receive a natural stimulus. In two years the Depression would be ended.

from V.W.F., "Men Versus Women", *Vancouver Through the Eyes of a Hobo*, 1934.

Top 1935. Kitsilano Yacht Club.

Bottom 1935. Interior of a house on North West Marine Drive in the University Hill area. Leonard Frank photograph.

Top 1938. Lions Gate Bridge nearing completion. Begun in 1936 it was almost named the Jubilee Bridge in commemoration of the city's Golden Jubilee.

Bottom 1932. Brockton Point in Stanley Park, Vancouver skyline in background. RCAF photograph.

Can it be true that the city is contemplating an outlay of $35,000 to put up a fountain in Lost Lagoon? A fountain!...

There are starving people in Vancouver, and hundreds of undernourished; there are dozens of useful things held up for lack of funds. There is no money for such things, but to spoil and ruin a natural loveliness like the Lost Lagoon there is apparently $35,000. Are we mad, gentlemen, or is it only spring coming!

from "Are We Mad?" 15 April 1936, Lost Lagoon Docket, Vancouver City Archives.

In this last year we in Vancouver have taken what appears to me to be a retrograde step. We have departed from the ward system and have reduced the number of elected representatives. The ward system...has the great advantage of ensuring the representation of all classes and of permitting the voters to select as their representatives people whom they have some opportunity of knowing.

from W.J. Barrett-Lennard, *Report on the Reorganization of Civic Administration of the City of Vancouver*, 9 December 1936.

As we cannot get the Doukobours to become good, decent, law-abiding citizens, why waste any further time and money on them? Their home port, Vladivostock, is easy of access — why not load up some tramp steamers and conclude the unprofitable experiment?

You cannot graft the Siberian crab apple on to the Douglas Fir.
Conclusive

from *The New Deal*, 23 April 1937.

Vancouver Jubilee Song

Hats off, Vancouver,
On your Golden Jubilee.
Hail, hail our pioneers;
We're proud to be
Allowed to see
And to celebrate
Your great day, Vancouver.
To the world you hold the key;
Let's make merry,
Come by auto, train and ferry,
To our Jubilee!

Fred Weaver and Andy Manson, 1936, additional MS. 74, volume 3, Vancouver City Archives.

Right 1932. Vancouver from the air,
looking east towards downtown. The
walls of the new Hotel Vancouver are up,
but the Hotel was not finished until 1939.

Pages 110, 111 Mid 1930s. Summer
crowds at English Bay.

The Great God Gable is no myth, but an actual creature of flesh and blood. That much has Vancouver learned; ladies of Vancouver, however, will not let such a minor detail drive them from their rites at the foot of his pedestal.

The hungry eyes of teenaged girls lurking in the hotel lobby for a glimpse of him; the souvenir-lust of married matrons who almost ruined his car in the hunt; the wildly-waving autograph books at the races; the scores who tried to crash the gate to his suite; showed that adulation waxes rather than wanes when cinematic shadows become reality.

from Monty Roberts, *The Vancouver Province*, 1933.

Because Pasquale Fiore, Italian-born violinist, refused to "destroy his art" by accepting employment to support his wife and seven Canadian-born children, he will spend one month in jail, where his surroundings will probably be far from artistic.

Today he was convicted on a charge of non-support after relief officials told how he refused relief employment, declaring that "pick and shovel" work would ruin his musical hands and discount him as a player of stringed instruments.

Witnesses said that when they visited his home...the man declared: "I won't do it. There is my work," and pointed to a musical score which he had been writing.

from "Violinist Who Refuses Work Goes to Jail", 6 August 1937, *Unemployment and Relief, City of Vancouver*, volume 8, number 54, Vancouver City Archives.

The fight for and against beer and wine in public dining-rooms is growing in intensity.... The big argument for the change, of course, is the present almost unrestricted sale of liquor in the United States. Already this has had a positive effect in British Columbia, according to information secured by the government. It is causing a steady flow of British Columbia tourists to the United States border towns, like Bellingham, to enjoy the thrill of dining in public with wine and beer, and it may reduce American travel here next summer, hotelmen say.

from "Beer Sale in Cafes Favored", 26 February 1934, Liquor Control Docket, Vancouver City Archives.

113

Vancouver broadcasting! Yes, those words are going to mean something within the next two months. After years in the background of Canadian radio, this city at last stands on the doorstep of a broadcasting era that will put the far-western link of the Dominion chain into a position that has been enjoyed by nearly every other major city in Canada.

from "Vancouver Going on Air in Big Way", *The Vancouver News-Herald*, 5 January 1937.

May I claim a small space in your progressive paper to refer to the traffic signals. They are a good thing, but the pedestrian, as he proceeds along the sidewalk, does not think of looking into the air to see the red light, hence finds himself often running against the law. Now, Sir, I think that the signals for the pedestrian should be shown on the sidewalk, so that it would check him up as he advances.
Progressive

from *The Vancouver News-Herald*, 5 May 1933.

Only the other day an old and respected couple employed as janitors in a city church informed me that their small monthly salary had been further reduced by five dollars in order that the managers might raise one thousand dollars as a special fund.... They told me that the church secretary had been laid off without pay, of course, but that when the minister returns from his vacation, he will receive a cheque for $250, being his month's pay. Now is this Christianity?

from James MacLeod, *The Vancouver News-Herald*, 8 July 1933.

Can any of your readers explain why I, in common with almost every member of the male sex I have approached on the subject, should have such an active dislike for the ultra-long and highly tinted fingernails adopted by the fashionable women of today?... I heartily approve of the various other items of make-up, such as rouge, lipstick, etc.... Yet the sight of those tapering, blood-red nails invariably gives me the shudders.

Maybe it is just an inherited distaste handed down from primitive times when the cave-woman matched her sharpened talons against the stone club of her mate!
G.W.

from "Fingernail Complaint", 10 March 1937, Games, Dances, Fashions Docket, Vancouver City Archives.

Left 1938. Policemen during the Post
Office riot.

Mr. Jenkinson: In 1938, that was the year of the famous sit-down strike of the unemployed in Vancouver. The Georgia Hotel and the Art Gallery were occupied by the unemployed....

Mr. Winch:...they just had nowhere to go and they had to try and compel the Governments to move into some form of action. So the way they did it at the start was three-fold. One, to take over a Federal Building so as to involve the Federal Government into action; so that was the Post Office. Then to bring the Provincial Government into it by hitting at the municipality, which is a child of the Provincial Government; so they moved into the Art Gallery. Three, to hit at the private enterprise system that was denying them the right to employment and the opportunity of employment; so they took over the Hotel Georgia.... Of course, the Aldermen and the acting Mayor were very much concerned, so they bought off the sit-downers in the Hotel Georgia... and they were there for a month in the Art Gallery and the Post Office.

from an interview with Mr. Harold Edward Winch, number 148, Oral History Programme, Reynoldston Research and Studies.

Evicted from quarters which they had occupied in the Post Office and Art Gallery for the past four weeks, the lawless element among 800 unemployed men ran riot in Vancouver on Sunday. At the end of a turbulent day 38 had been admitted to hospital, 23 were locked in the city jail and the downtown business district had suffered damage estimated in excess of $50,000.... Fleeing before a barrage of tear gas bombs and the swinging batons of city police officers, a swarm of shouting, blood-spattered men smashed hundreds of plate glass windows, looted stores, and for more than an hour created a reign of terror in the city.

from "800 Sitdowners Stage Riot; 23 Jailed, 100 Men Hurt", *The Vancouver News-Herald*, 20 June 1938.

Top 1938. Evacuation of sit-down strikers from the Post Office at Granville and Hastings streets.

Bottom 22 June 1938. Unemployed "tin canners".

Top 1933. *Vancouver Sun* yo-yo contest. Stuart Thomson photograph.

Bottom ca. 1937. Plaza Theatre on Granville Street. Marquee reads "Assassin of youth - exposes those wild Marihuana parties. Passions unleashed by innocent fun". Stuart Thomson photograph.

I've always dreaded long, tedious trips. Sure, I knew planes would save hours — even days — but I never associated flying with my own travel needs....

Now *I'm* going to know what it's like to be in one of those mighty Flagships—to eat a meal a mile or so above the ground, to "turn in" on a berth as wide as a twin bed and a full six feet, five inches long—to sleep under the stars and dream my way across the continent.

from *American Airlines*, Inc. advertisement, 1 June 1938.

In self defence city electrician's department may have to recommend the setting apart of a "Lovers' Lane" where only the moon will add its romantic light to moments of bliss.

It may sound farcical, but Vancouver appears to be so short of shady nooks that lovesick swains have been compelled to create desirable spots by the simple expedient of smashing globes and lamps on the overhead standards. They have been doing their courting at the expense of the ratepayers....

While Chief Constable W.W. Foster suggested there should be streets specially reserved for spooners, Ald. Fred Crone proposed "No Parking—No Necking" signs might be posted.

from "Cupid Throws Rocks At Electric Light Globes In 'Necking' Nooks", 16 April 1938, Traffic Docket 2, Vancouver City Archives.

Thrills, chills and spills were supplied generously to Vancouver residents at Brighouse Park on Tuesday evening, as two dare-devil drivers, Tommy Mantle and Warren Lapierre, staged the Chrysler "Hell-Drivers" show....

The show reached its climax when a car was rolled over twice before the stands. The driver then waited until a field-crew had righted the automobile, and drove it away. Front fenders and bonnet were crumpled in this demonstration of the steel-body safety, but the body of the car was scarcely dented.

from "Hell Drivers Thrill Crowd", 18 August 1937, Games, Dances, Fashions Docket, Vancouver City Archives.

The Lambeth Walk! Everybody's doing the Lambeth Walk. It's sweeping the country and swept the Spanish Grill Saturday evening when Mart Kenney instructed a gay throng of revellers in the not-so-intricate new dance, on the opening night of his winter engagement.

from "Vancouver Steps Out; Dancing Rendezvous Popular", *The Vancouver News-Herald*, 24 October 1938.

There is a present craze among the younger folk for disfiguring themselves by wearing dark glasses with colored celluloid rims.

Origin of the fad is easily traced to a desire to emulate stars of the movie colony at Hollywood. Beginning with a pseudo-smart set it has spread to include high school students and other vigorous young animals of that age.

I will be set down as a cranky old mossback, but I cannot see a single reason why this hideous fad should be perpetrated.

from "Man With a Lantern", *The Vancouver Sun*, 22 June 1938.

Woman had no sooner emancipated herself from the dust gathering skirt—and she deserves the highest praise for a step that required no little courage—that she must draw her skirts up over her knees with the excuse that it gives her freedom of action. She wears the most abbreviated shorts on the tennis court and tries to fool herself and her friends that she can dart from the baseline to the net with greater freedom because her limbs are untrammelled.

from George Wright, "Casual Comments", *The Vancouver News-Herald*, 20 August 1937.

Information has reached the United Church of Canada that bingo and similar games are the spearhead of a national movement to "pry open the Criminal Code" to allow lotteries and other forms of gambling, Rev. E.S. Bishop, social service committee chairman, said at yesterday's meeting of Toronto East Presbytery. Mr. Bishop said the movement started in Vancouver.

from " 'Bingo' to Popularize Gambling, Says Minister", 3 March 1937, Games Docket, Vancouver City Archives.

BO-LO BILLY
Says:

"It's smart to buy your Bo-Lo at THE BAY and have the champion teach you how to play it FREE OF CHARGE!"

HAROLD COVENT, world's champion BO-LO player, will put on a fascinating show of Bo-Lo Tricks on Saturday from 9 to 12 noon. He will also make several appearances during the afternoon. Stationery Department, Main Floor.

Hudson's Bay Company.
INCORPORATED 2ᵗʰ MAY 1670.

1939. Living room of suite in the newly opened Hotel Vancouver at Georgia and Burrard streets. Stuart Thomson photograph.

I noticed your article on the front page of the Sun Monday, in which you summarize the dangerous driving in Vancouver and also the futility of attempting to drive at thirty miles an hour without being a subject of insults from other drivers.

I drove down from Kerrisdale this morning at thirty miles an hour, slowing down at intersections. I was passed by thirty-four cars, I received twelve honks to pull into the right, I received nine dirty looks—two of these looks may not have been intended but were probably the drivers' natural expressions.

from "What is Your Opinion", *The Vancouver Sun*, 10 July 1939.

Mass excitement which became almost tangible in its intensity before each difficult feat...staccato thunder in the clap of white-gloved hands...a shepherd's check pattern of black and white formality in boxes filled to capacity...the brilliant first night of the Vancouver Horseshow lived up to its promise of unique entertainment in the city's annals of equestrian exhibition.

Seldom equalled as a colorful scene, the horseshow drew an audience of highly social significance. Top-hatted gentlemen ringed each box, their ladies smartly formal in glittering evening gowns under luxurious wraps of ermine and velvet. White furs were decidedly the favorite choice, expressed in the majority by the short hip-length models of the 1938 season.

from "Equestrian Display Attracts Brilliant Audience", 22 November 1938, Horse Show Building Docket, Vancouver City Archives.

"Don't Send Bombs for Christmas"; "Munitions Sent to Japan Will Return Someday"; "Are You Helping Bring Peace on Earth".

Those were the terse messages on some of the hundreds of banners, placards and sandwich boards carried through the streets of Vancouver all day Wednesday by sympathizers with the Embargo Council that sponsored a "Peaceful Protest Walk" to show their disapproval of shipments of scrap iron from this port to Japan.

from "Arms Embargo Paraders Are Well Received by Citizens", 22 December 1938, Japanese Docket 1, Vancouver City Archives.

Are You An Accomplice In This Crime?

TO THE SHOPPER AND HOUSEWIFE:

Do you know that you are helping to kill innocent men, women and children in China when you purchase goods made in Japan? Now that Christmas is coming—the season of Goodwill upon Earth—do you wish to be a partner in the crimes being committed by the Japanese war-machine? Help us to bring Peace on Earth by taking the bullets out of Japanese guns that are bringing death to the Chinese people!

TO ALL CITIZENS:

When you fail to protest to the Dominion Government against the shipment of nickel, copper, scrap iron and other war materials to Japan you, too, are guilty of murder in the second degree by being a silent partner in the slaughter of innocent Chinese people, who are your good friends and neighbors across the Pacific.

TO THE BUSINESS MAN:

When you buy from Japan or sell to Japan you are helping to destroy Canada's finest market and your own business future. A free and democratic China will buy Canadian products. Japan, if victorious, will close the OPEN DOOR and drive the white business man from Asiatic markets!

HUMANITY AND YOUR OWN BUSINESS INTERESTS DEMAND COMPLETE BOYCOTT OF ALL GOODS MADE IN JAPAN!

Issued by
THE MEDICAL AID FOR CHINA COMMITTEE

Provincial Office: 615 WEST HASTINGS STREET, VANCOUVER, B. C.

Left May 1939. Hastings Street decorated for the visit of King George VI and Queen Elizabeth, a few days before the outbreak of World War II. Sign on David Spencer's store says "Long Live the King". Leonard Frank photograph.

On to Victory
1939–1945

Canada entered World War II on 10 September 1939. Vancouver's long climb out of the Depression was accelerated by the war, and by 1941 the economy was healthy enough to provoke a building boom that set local records. But development slowed to a crawl when wartime industries in full production began to absorb all available supplies and labour. For the first time since World War I, the demand for workers outstripped the demand for employment. The working woman of the Depression, that wanton creature intent on stealing men's jobs, was rehabilitated as a wartime heroine of the most necessary kind. Women began driving buses and took their places in the shipyards and in the Boeing aircraft factory on Sea Island beside workers from the prairies and the B.C. Interior.

Military headquarters were set up in the old Hotel Vancouver at Georgia and Granville, and the Navy and Air Force expanded their bases at Kitsilano, Sea Island and Jericho Beach. In 1943 the Navy opened a training base on Deadman's Island. Hundreds of pilots learned to fly at the airport, which the Dominion government leased from the city in 1940 and enlarged by 250 acres. But the rest of Vancouver still watched the war from the benches.

All that changed on 7 December 1941, when the Japanese attacked Pearl Harbor and blackout precautions were enforced for several days as a wave of panic swept the Pacific coast. Although the only attack on British Columbia was the shelling of Estevan lighthouse on the west coast of Vancouver Island on 20 June 1942, the lack of a serious threat did nothing to divert suspicion from the Japanese in Vancouver. The federal government took what it considered appropriate measures, placing the city's 9,000-member Japanese community and some 14,000 additional Japanese living on the coast under immediate restriction, including registration and a curfew. Even these measures, which did not apply to resident Germans or Italians (also enemy aliens), failed to reassure anti-Japanese British Columbians. Under pressure from the local press and politicians, all Japanese were moved to detention camps at the end of March 1942.

As the war went on, the city began to show signs of strain. Beginning in September 1942, rationing was imposed on a list of products including sugar, butter, liquor, coffee, tea and gasoline. Potholes stayed in the streets, and sewers, water mains and parks got a minimum of attention. Despite the completion of both Patullo and Lion's Gate bridges in 1938 the newly accessible suburbs they served showed only modest growth. By August 1944 there was an acute housing shortage, with 2,000 units urgently needed to house war workers and their families.

By V-J Day, 14 August 1945, Vancouver was ready to relax and celebrate. The neglect of the Depression and the war years had left a gray and dowdy city, but this shabbiness paled beside the rubble of Europe. Vancouver welcomed home its returning soldiers, rejoiced in having escaped the destruction of the war and reached out eagerly for the fruits of postwar prosperity.

Within a day of Britain's declaration of war against Germany the way of Canadian life has been altered. The country was calm Sunday—but nobody smiled. It was Labor Day week-end, the last long holiday week-end of summer, but Canadians had no appetite for carefree holidaying. Churches were crowded. Millions sat beside radios from early morning until late night. They heard Mr. Chamberlain, the King, Premier Daladier, Mr. Mackenzie King, and his ministers explain the position of Empire and Canada.

from "Canada Receives News Calmly; Recruiting Stations Crowded", *The Vancouver Sun*, 4 September 1939.

Four days of intensive applications for marriage licences, due to military mobilization, resulted in the Vancouver registry district receiving about 250 applications. This record is unique in its history, officials stated at closing hour Friday.

from "Marriage Licence Rush", *The Vancouver News-Herald*, 9 September 1939.

Far-seeing housewives gave Vancouver its first taste of food-hoarding Friday when hundreds of them flocked to city stores to lay in reserve stocks of eatables. Particularly were they concerned with laying away supplies of sugar. Many of the women were seen with handy men in tow, lugging 100-pound sacks to waiting automobiles.

from "Food Hoarding Starts in Vancouver," *The Vancouver News-Herald*, 2 September 1939.

Ten thousand women are working in B.C. war industries and, within a year, 20,000 will be employed....

It may be news to most people, but men are leaving Vancouver war industries to return to logging camps. The lumber shortage has resulted in such attractive terms for loggers that war industries can not compete....

Appreciation of war industries for women workers is increasing. Their "stability" and "efficiency in repetitive jobs" are gaining "growing recognition for them."

from "Supply of Single Women for B.C. War Industries", *The Vancouver Daily Province*, 6 November 1942.

Page 120 1 October 1940. "Wait for me, Daddy". The British Columbia Regiment, Duke of Connaught's Own, marching down Eighth Street in New Westminster prior to embarkation for overseas. C.P. Dettloff photograph.

Top left 1945. Women workers in Wallace Shipyards.

Bottom left Boeing airplane plant on Sea Island. Jack Lindsay photograph.

Top 1942. Japanese men at the CNR station on their way to internment camps.

Bottom 18 May 1942. Children's dining room in Hastings Park where the Japanese were gathered prior to internment. Leonard Frank photograph.

British Columbia went to war against Japan Sunday a few minutes after the first bombs fell on Honolulu and the Phillipines....

R.C.M.P. and Provincial Police swiftly rounded up dangerous enemy aliens while spokesmen for British Columbia's 24,000 Japanese declared their unswerving allegiance to Canada. Japanese language schools and newspapers were closed. A roundup of the Japanese fishing fleet, which will be immobilized, was under way.

from "City On War Basis As Pacific Erupts", 8 December 1941, Japanese Docket 2, Vancouver City Archives.

Get home as soon as possible tonight—and stay there. Use the telephone as infrequently as possible. There are emergency calls waiting to get through. There must be no light escaping from your home and it is your responsibility to test your own blackout precautions. Your head lights must be blinded except for a vertical slit three inches long and one-quarter inch wide. Tail-lights must be blinded except for a small disc in the centre.

from "Must...and...Please", *The Vancouver News-Herald*, 10 December 1941.

We Canadians have reached a point where we must stop and think deeply regarding our evacuation.... We have said "YES" to all your previous orders, however unreasonable they might have seemed. But we are firm in saying "NO" to your last order which calls for the break-up of our families.

When we say "NO" at this point, we request you to remember that we are British subjects by birth, that we are no less loyal to Canada than any other Canadian, that we have done nothing to deserve the break-up of our families, that we are law-abiding Canadian citizens and that we are willing to accept suspension of our civil rights—rights to retain our homes and businesses, boats, cars, radios, and cameras.... In view of this sacrifice we feel that our request for mass evacuation in family groups will not seem unreasonable to you.

Respectfully yours,
Nisei Mass Evacuation Group.

from letter to Austin C. Taylor, 15 April 1942, in Halford Wilson papers, additional MS. 12, volume 2/10, B.C. Provincial Archives.

Nearly $1,000,000 in Japanese real property will have been sold in Vancouver on completion of the federal government's compulsory sale order.... Approximately half of the 464 parcels of property ordered sold have already been disposed of.... Household furniture, appliances and other chattels owned by the evacuee Japanese are now being sold at public auction.... Already sold are the Japanese fishing boats, autos, trucks, and virtually all of their business operations.

from "Jap Property Sales in City Net Owners Near $1,000,000", *The Vancouver Daily Province*, 19 May 1944.

What happened to effigies of Hitler and Mussolini last night shouldn't happen to a witch. Four thousand excited spectators milled around a giant fire and watched 50 foot flames lick at the feet of Hitler's and Mussolini's stuffed dummies, as the second annual community Halloween celebration, sponsored by the North Vancouver Parent Teachers' Association was held.

from "Mussolini and Hitler Burn as Kiddies Howl with Glee", *The Vancouver Daily Province*, 1 November 1941.

The one-third reduction in the butter rationing, announced on Wednesday, was taken right on the chin, without a single murmur, by the housewives of Vancouver.

A survey of women in the city showed, on Wednesday, that they were quite prepared to accept whatever amount of butter the government saw fit to apportion to them.

Miss A. Glassbran of Chilco Street said: "I would say we were a pack of pikers if we even say one word about the reduction in butter rationing. We are lucky to have any at all. When we think of all the things the Britishers are doing without, the least we can do is use a little less butter. I think we are very lucky as we are now."

from "We'll Manage — Wives Answer to Reduction in Butter Ration", 21 January 1942, Butter Docket, Vancouver City Archives.

The wartime shortage of metals is going to cramp the style of Canada's skiers, fishermen and golfers — especially golfers.

from "Metal Shortage Hard on Sport", *The Vancouver Sun*, 5 March 1942.

Top 1941. Woodward's food department.

Bottom February 1943. Queen Mary School in North Vancouver, first school in the Vancouver area to carry out air raid drill equipped with gas masks.

EVERY RIVET A BULLET

SPEED THE SHIPS

IT'S EASY TO SEE WHO USES **ODEX** SOAP BEFORE COMING TO SCHOOL!

Only 6¢

Vancouver's cabbages and potatoes are to be marching with its troops this coming summer. Its Victory Gardens are to be on parade.... Victory Gardens can be definitely lined up as a war effort, for every potato grown in the backyard will be one less mother will have to buy at the store, one more the wholesaler will have available to turn over to the army.

from " 'Victory Gardeners' Army to be 40,000 Strong", *The Vancouver News-Herald*, 16 February 1943.

Vancouver's housing shortage is forcing many families to use auto trailers as homes until they are able to purchase or build a house. One couple have occupied a trailer for a year.

from " 'City on Wheels' Rising Here", *The Vancouver Daily Province*, 9 May 1944.

The Police Commission Friday, after hearing evidence of drunkenness and "lewd embraces" in Vancouver cabarets from eyewitnesses who reported on their investigations, instructed police to enforce the closing of cabarets every night of the week at 1 a.m....

Mrs. D.M. McKay, a member of a delegation representing the Local Council of Women....said that bottles of liquor were kept on the floor in the earlier part of the evening, but later were passed openly across the table and glasses were left in full view.

She described "nice girls" intoxicated, engaging in "lewd embraces and long kisses," and said that before the closing hour virtually everyone was drunk and "couples were embracing all over the room." The floor show she described as "objectionable," with girls "naked except for brassieres and loin cloths."

from "Police Revert to One O'Clock Cabaret Closing", *The Vancouver News-Herald*, 13 December 1941.

If you have been going bare-legged you've probably experimented with a number of different leg makeups. The bottled chiffon, a survey reveals, is used by 93 per cent of women, cake-leg makeups by 5 per cent and the stick or cream pastes by 2 per cent.

from "Pointers on Leg Makeup", 29 July 1944, Games, Dances, Fashions Docket 1, Vancouver City Archives.

I know why Ottawa wants to chlorinate our water. Jealousy! One finds sometimes in families an unnatural mother will be most unpleasantly jealous of a daughter's beauty and development. British Columbia is growing up and becoming important, so Ottawa says: "Darn you; I'll spoil your famous water for you, anyway." If Vancouver or any part of the lower mainland had an air raid and really cut a figure in the world's press, the entire East would turn pea-green with envy.
Reader

from "Ottawa Jealous?" *The Vancouver Sun*, 11 September 1942.

License Inspector H.A. Urquhart revealed on Monday that he has used the city license by-law in recent months to ban boisterous dancing to juke box music in more than a dozen hamburger joints and soft drink parlors.

from "Clamp on Suburban Night Spots", 18 November 1943, Juke Boxes Docket, Vancouver City Archives.

Kitsies, when interviewed as to what they think of Frank Sinatra, lay him low with a two to one vote. Only one-third of the staff and students appear to favor this new feature of the radio and phonograph. In general, female Kitsies consider his voice good but will not consider him as Frank Swoonatra.

from *Kitsilano High School Life*, volume 15, number 2, December 1943.

The Vancouver edition of the "zoot-suiters" ranges from 15 to 17 years of age. He wears a jacket which comes down almost to his knees in many cases. His trousers are baggy in the seat, but so tight at the cuff that shoes have to be removed to get the trousers on or off.

He either wears bright-colored socks, no socks at all, or mismatched ones. The shirt under the jacket may be any style, even a sweat shirt. His hair is long.

In extreme cases, not common here, he wears a pork-pie hat with wide brim and sports a heavy watch chain which dangles almost to the ground.

from *The Vancouver Daily Province*, 1 August 1944.

The "SALAD SALUTE" that says Welcome Home!

BEST FOODS

Real Mayonnaise

REALLY FRESH

AINSLIE & CO., LTD. • Distributors
VANCOUVER, B.C.

Tell NOBODY — not even HER

CARELESS TALK COSTS LIVES

At long last the government has awakened to the fact that the Canadian Universities (to a large extent at least) have for the past four years been acting as "shelters" for young men of perfect physical health, but apparently deficient in nerve and moral calibre.

But why not make the dragnet more effective still. Crowds of husky young giants have fled to unskilled labor in shipyards and other works, simply to escape the more serious work of taking up arms for their country.

Conscription for service anywhere seems to be the only solution. "May it come now" is the fervent wish of tens of thousands.

U.B.C. and Vimy Veteran

from *the Vancouver Daily Province*, 27 August 1943.

Victory Day (last Feb. 21) which saw three 10,000-ton steel cargo ships launched in Port of Vancouver yards alone, was "only the beginning, folks, only the beginning." Because four more steel freighters — the kind of ships so important in the maintenance of allied lines of communication and supply in this world-wide war — will slide down the ways in Vancouver shipyards before the end of March, I learned today. And that's important news...because it proves that the shipbuilding industry on the Pacific Coast of Canada has really started to roll.

from Don Mason, "City Yards to Launch Four Ships This Month", *The Vancouver Sun*, 4 March 1942.

Vancouver mothers today flocked to banks and department stores to cash their family allowance cheques. Many of them opened bank accounts for their children and deposited the money in trust for them.

The new accounts development was noticed particularly in the west and southwest parts of the city; in the eastern section, bankers said, "Few of the mothers are opening new accounts. Mostly they are just cashing the cheques."

from "Mothers Flock to Cash 'Baby Bonus' Cheques", *The Vancouver Daily Province*, 20 July 1945.

Top left Troops embarking. Marine Building in the background. Jack Lindsay photograph.

Bottom left Landing exercises at Kitsilano Beach. Jack Lindsay photograph.

Parade passing in front of the Banff Apartments, at the corner of Georgia and Bute streets. Jack Lindsay photograph.

15 August 1945. V-J Day celebrations.

Right 15 August 1945. V-J Day
celebrations. Jack Lindsay photograph.

The large scale lay-offs of women from war
industries in B.C. in the latter months of
1944, and the difficulties of these women in
finding other satisfactory employment,
created a distinct feeling of uncertainty as to
the future of women in employment
generally....

Miss Elsie Silk, a former employee of the
Dominion Bridge Company, spoke on
behalf of girls no longer needed in war
plants. These girls became highly trained
and efficient — they could work to the
measurement of one-thousandth part of an
inch as easily as most women did sewing and
knitting. It was a loss to the nation not to use
this skill in the post-war period....

The general discussion brought out the
fact that there was no actual planning for
women's employment after the war; that the
general attitude was that women could be
called upon in a crisis, and that when the
crisis was over they would have to accept
whatever came....

from "The Future of Women in Employment", Report of
Conference held under the auspices of the Women's School
for Citizenship, 20 January 1945.

Some laughed, some were reflectively sober.
Many walked uncertainly out of the open
doors of Plant 3 to gaze in the direction of
the siren which shattered the sunlit
afternoon to tell the inhabitants and workers
of Sea Island that the war with Japan had
come to an end.

from "Japs Ask Peace Fourteen Months After First B-29
Raid", *Boeing Beam*, 31 August 1945.

Mr. and Mrs. Mount Pleasant, with
grandfather and grandmother and all the
little Pleasants — right down to those who sat
on Dad's shoulder or lay in Mother's arms —
drifted gradually to Tenth, between
Kingsway and Main, on V-J night.
There... community singing, street dancing
and just plain onlooking were enjoyed.
Everyone took part, from the 2-year-olds...to
pint-sized jitterbugs and veterans of World
War I.

from "Mount Pleasant Turns Loose", 15 August 1945, Mt.
Pleasant Docket 2, Vancouver City Archives.

1958. Somewhere in North Vancouver.
Fred Herzog photograph.

Crewcuts & Chrome
1945–1960

With the end of the war, Vancouver began the most sustained expansion in its history, outgrowing for the first time the shape that had been determined in the golden years of the century's first decade. Although the war industries began to close down late in 1944, sending thousands of women workers home to apply their energies to the baby boom, demand for British Columbia's resources remained high and Vancouver's economy prospered.

The good times brought people, swelling the population from 374,000 in 1941 to 562,000 in 1951. The central city grew, but its share of the total population fell from 79 per cent in 1941 to 48 per cent in 1961 as outlying areas picked up the growth. In the age of the private car, the once distant farming communities of Richmond, Delta, Surrey, Ladner and Coquitlam became commuter suburbs.

The city built new and larger bridges in a vain attempt to move more cars more quickly. Traffic to the Sea Island Airport and Richmond flowed over the Oak Street Bridge, built in 1957, then farther south through the Deas Island (now Massey) Tunnel, opened two years later. The old Second Narrows Bridge was replaced in 1960 with a new span designed to lure some of the North Shore traffic from congested Lion's Gate Bridge. Streetcars yielded to trolley buses. The old interurban railway stopped running in 1954 when the present Granville Street Bridge was opened without a train track in any of its eight lanes.

Vancouver grew up as well as out. The old Sun-World Tower, once the tallest building in the British Empire, was dwarfed by such skyscrapers as the B.C. Hydro building, itself a landmark only until 1957 when a change in zoning opened the West End to apartment towers. Large scale capital investment in the resource industries forced small lumber mills and fish canneries out of business or into mergers with the remaining giants. On the other side of an increasingly clear line, labour unions struggled for better wages and working conditions, using tactics that included some of the bitterest strikes in the city's history.

In the postwar climate of racial tolerance, the municipal vote was extended to all citizens of Asiatic origin, including the Japanese. The city became more cosmopolitan: by 1960 one resident in six was from continental Europe.

The strongest cultural pull of the 1950s came from the south, from American television and its nightly dose of continentalism. When the CBC began broadcasting in 1953, Vancouverites had already watched the coronation of Queen Elizabeth II on KVOS, the Bellingham station. By the time she arrived in person six years later to open the theatre named in her honour, Vancouver not only shared American culture but also suffered in a mild form the physical ills of any large North American city: traffic congestion, pollution, urban sprawl and a decaying city core.

Late 1940s. Georgia and Howe streets,
showing the old Hotel Vancouver and a
corner of the new Hotel. Jack Lindsay
photograph.

The City Council has a splendid opportunity to set a Jubilee example to every Vancouver property owner by setting aside $10,000 in its 1946 budget for beautifying the City Hall grounds this spring.

Visitors have long wondered why the city built a $1,000,000 City Hall but left it in a ten-cent setting.

from "Let's Spruce Up", 10 January 1946, Diamond Jubilee Docket, Vancouver City Archives.

Liquor Commissioner W.F. Kennedy said today there is a possibility liquor rationing will end later this year on all brands with the exception of imported Scotch whisky, but he added the prediction could be upset if supplies of bottles and cartons are cut.

Dealing with the campaign here for returning liquor to its pre-war strength, Mr. Kennedy declared that everyone in Canada who is connected with the industry is strongly against such a move.

from "Kennedy Supports Weakened Liquor: 'Everyone in the Business' Wants It", *The Vancouver Daily Province*, 28 January 1947.

Flood-swollen waters of the Fraser River have cut off Vancouver and the Lower Fraser Valley from all rail and road communication with the Interior and the rest of Canada....

Hundreds of persons are pouring into Vancouver from badly-hit Aggassiz, Harrison and Nicomen Island. More are going to Abbotsford and Mission.

No flood in the history of the valley has endangered more life and property than the present ever-rising crest that is the result of more than average snowfall in the vast mountainous Fraser watershed. Checked by a late spring, the floods now pouring seaward have not yet reached a peak.

from "Rail, Road Links Cut; Disaster Faces Valley", *The Vancouver Daily Province*, 29 May 1948.

Right Late 1940s. Teddy Lyons conducting a tour on the B.C. Electric Railway Observation Car, Robson Street. The service ended in 1950 after 40 years of operation. Jack Lindsay photograph.

Late 1940s. Reddy Kilowatt sign outside B.C. Electric appliance showroom. Jack Lindsay photograph.

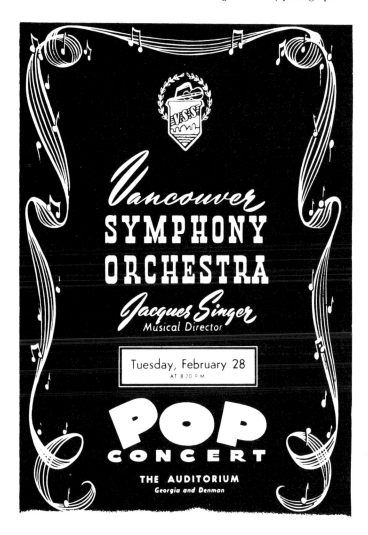

Vancouver drivers who figure the old "my doctor gave me a pill" gag is wearing a bit thin should try telling the magistrate they were hypnotized. Unless, that is, they have to face a drunkometer.

B.C. Fleet Supervisors' Association, demonstrating Seattle's Harger breath tester...found Wednesday night that only the machine can tell the difference between a real drunk and a man under hypnosis. They fed driving school chief Bill McKinley half a "26" of rye and hypnotized truck driver Ed Palmer.

Even Vancouver's Assistant Chief Harry Whelan admitted he couldn't really be sure which was which. But the machine recorded Mr. McKinley drunk and Mr. Palmer cold sober.

from "Drunkometer Can Tell About Hypnotism, Too", 6 December 1951, Drunkometer Docket, Vancouver City Archives.

There are pirates on Lost Lagoon in Stanley Park. Mostly they just steal free boating time. But they have been known to attempt to row off with the boats they rent at the Lagoon float. Only one boat rustler has ever been successful, and that was in 1949.

The boat rustlers usually are spotted as they attempt to sneak the boat out of the park. In the chase that ensues the boat is dropped and the would-be thieves take to their heels.

from "Rowboat 'Pirates' On Lost Lagoon", *The Vancouver Sun*, 13 March 1953.

Detective-Sergeant Len Cuthbert testified Thursday that in 1949 he split graft money from two "east end" bookmakers with Police Chief Walter Mulligan, and received from the chief a share of pay-off money from West End bookies. Cuthbert's sensational evidence before the police royal commission, which resumed after a 14-day adjournment, bore out predictions that he would "tell all" when he entered the witness box. A packed, hushed courtroom heard the long-awaited evidence of Cuthbert, who appeared calm but weak from the effects of his self-inflicted bullet wound and of weeks of anxiety and tension.

from "Cuthbert Tells Inquiry He Split Pay offs from East End Bookies with Mulligan", *The Vancouver News-Herald*, 29 July 1955.

Right Late 1940s. Panorama from City Hall. Jack Lindsay photograph.

139

Hundreds of Vancouver Chinese are beginning to realize a dream which began in far-off China 20 years ago. Their wives and children are coming to Canada at last. Lifting of the prohibitory Chinese Immigration Act and PC 1378 two years ago signalled the end of a narrow existence in dingy exclusively male tenements along Shanghai Alley and Hong Kong Street.

In the past few months between 300 and 400 wives and children of Chinese Canadians have arrived in Vancouver. Many more have continued their journey to other parts of Canada.

from "Dream Comes True For City Chinese", 12 December 1949, Chinese Docket 4, Vancouver City Archives.

Tall apartment buildings, of ten storeys or more, will start rising over English Bay within the next five years. They will mark the second stage of an architectural revolution unique in Vancouver, and so far peculiar to the West End. The first stage is well under way. It has already changed the area west of Denman. It involves the building of modern, steel-and-concrete apartment blocks rising from three to six storeys.... The apartment house, once associated with cramped quarters, tenement conditions and a general lowering of residential standards, is now a symbol of rejuvenation.

from D'arcy Marsh, "West End Starts Unique Comeback", *The Vancouver Sun*, 30 March 1953.

The object of "Downtown Day" was to counteract the growing tendency for housewives to shop in the suburban centres, where almost everything adequate can now be purchased.... It was the worst sort of failure. At 10 a.m. Friday, Dec. 8th, the streets were "deserted" and the stores were empty; there were fewer people than usual, and the extra buses were empty.

from J.S. Matthews, "Downtown Day: the First, 1951", December 1951, Downtown Docket, Vancouver City Archives.

Left 1949. Demolition of the old Hotel Vancouver at Georgia and Granville streets. Bill Cunningham photograph.

Top 1949. Children play in the alley near tenements on West 2nd Avenue.

Bottom Late 1940s. Traffic on Kingsway.

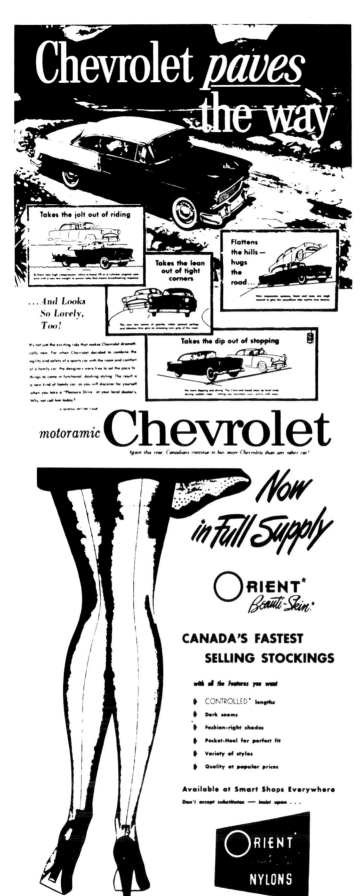

Skidroad is where Vancouver fades into shabby, shadowy sordidness. It is where the derelicts of a great city dwell in filthy jungles, only a few blocks from main streets. The oily smell of the vast waterfront mingles with the stench of the city dump and the odor of stale alcohol....

Men comprise 90 per cent of the Skidroad population. In the Wonder Lunch, which has served the district for 50 years, "No Women Served" signs warn predatory females, looking for a pick-up, to beware. Few women live in Skidroad.

from Cy Young, "Skidroad", *Weekend Picture Magazine*, 1 December 1951.

So far in 1954, Vancouver has had an average of more than one death every three days as a result of domestic gas poisoning.

from "Death Every Three Days City's 1954 Gas Toll", 27 January 1954, Gas Docket, Vancouver City Archives.

The real hoodlum gangs, often unrecognized as such in their own neighborhood, are generally identified by their ridiculous strides, voluminous pants cut in a Dutch drape. They measure up to 36 inches across the knee, narrow abruptly to 14 around the ankle, have a three-to-five corset waist and a high English rise in the back....

Some members of the Burnaby gang...have adopted crew cuts and a cut known in various gang areas as an "Iroquois" or a "Huron", which is a skull shaven except for a strip down the middle.

from Mac Reynolds, "10-12 Vicious Gangs In City", *The Vancouver Sun*, 23 January 1950.

Gangs of street hoodlums, roaming the Point Grey and Kerrisdale residential districts by the thousands last night, taunted the full might of the Vancouver police force with showers of rotten eggs, caused property damage impossible to estimate, and gave the city its worst Halloween vandalism orgy in years.

Worst offenders were the teen-age youths of the Kerrisdale and Shaughnessy district, who jammed the streets at Forty-first and Granville and held up traffic for most of the early evening.

from *The Vancouver Sun*, 1 November 1946.

Vancouver's "iron curtain" against race, color and creed has been raised slightly — but certainly not demolished—by the Supreme Court of Canada decision upholding sale of property to a Jew.

Groups of Jews, Chinese, Negroes and East Indians...felt the upholding of their rights by the highest court should give pause to property owners in Shaughnessy, Kerrisdale, Capilano Highlands, Westmount and British Properties who enforce such discrimination.

from "Jews Hail Court Ruling, But Doubt Its Effect", 21 November 1950, Jews Docket 2, Vancouver City Archives.

An endless stream of bananas is pouring from the holds of the United Fruit Co. SS. Comayagua, at Ballantyne, slowed perhaps, by the fact that the longshoremen are eyeing all stems with caution of possible deadly snakes and spiders.

It is no nice feeling for a Canadian longshoreman to feel the cold coils of a serpent around his arm, or the feet of a spider crawling over his chest.

from "Longshoremen Move Gingerly As Snake Appears in Bananas", 21 June 1947, Bananas Docket, Vancouver City Archives.

Canada's first backyard atomic bomb shelter has been built on a side lawn on Shaughnessy Heights.... The woman who will own the steel-reinforced shelter for four people does not want her name mentioned because publicity on the project has caused people "to pester me to death."

from *The Vancouver Sun*, 29 August 1950.

Vancouver will sample the world's first commercial frozen apple juice concentrate at the end of this month. It will be B.C.-made from B.C. apples by B.C. Fruit Processors Ltd.

from "World's First Frozen Apple Juice for City", 17 January 1951, Apples Docket, Vancouver City Archives.

Only yesterday, 20 students jammed themselves into the Quad phone booth to establish a world record. The record was formerly held by North Staffordshire University College, Keele, England, who squeezed 17 into a booth thus taking the title from Manchester University who only managed 16.

from *The Ubyssey*, 7 March 1959.

Top May 1956. Four-way traffic comes to a halt for pedestrians at Georgia and Granville.

Bottom ca. 1950 Kitsilano Secondary School vocal ensemble group.

Vancouver's man-on-the-street believed Princess Margaret should marry the man she loves and to heck with tradition.... Margaret's name has been linked romantically with several suitors. But most recently and most seriously, as far as the Royal Family is concerned, is that of Peter Townsend — a divorced commoner.

from "City Residents Say Margaret Should Marry Man She Loves", *The Vancouver Sun*, 17 August 1955.

Pelvis Prediction — If Elvis Presley ever dares set foot back in Vancouver for a singing engagement he'll have to warble at the corner of Granville and Georgia. As far as Pacific National officials are concerned he can't come back into Empire Stadium or any other part of the PNE. Orders to stop the show were given by PNE officials when the mob got out of hand.... Dueck's wouldn't let Elvis ride around the track in their Caddie until the car firm was assured that the singer carried insurance against mob violence.

from Jack Wasserman, "About Now", 3 September 1957, PNE Docket, Vancouver City Archives.

UBC students have joined Toronto and Cambridge students in hitting out at Red-baiting Sen. Joseph McCarthy and Col. Robert R. McCormick's English-baiting *Chicago Tribune*. Campus clubs denounced McCarthy for his "witch-hunting" tactics, calling the Republican senator a "fascist" and telling him to "stay out of Canada."

from "Students Tell Joe 'No Help Wanted' ", *The Ubyssey*, 10 November 1953.

Music is fun. Rock and roll or a slow waltz, there are people for every style. But some folks on a bus like to have a quiet peaceful moment to think. They would be grateful if you would switch your portable radios off while on buses.

from "Don't Rock Buses", *The Buzzer*, 17 October 1958.

Garish gobs of color, sombre shading, recognizable landscapes and portraits, and completely incomprehensible blotches of paint line the walls of four rooms of the gallery. Painters there — Picasso, Leger, Klee, Modigliani, Matisse — are the men who 40 years ago set the artistic world on its ear. Some of the artists who visited the show Monday said they considered the argument between "representational" and "modern" was settled almost 40 years ago.

Maybe.

from Don Stainsby, "Guggenheim 'Art' Display Leaves Critics in Tizzy", *The Vancouver Sun*, 17 November 1954.

What's all this fuss about the Symphony Society, whether it shall have a dozen or so concerts or 50? Music is desirable in its place, and I personally prefer the so-called classics (dreadful, snobbish word) to the juke-box stuff. But I'm also a taxpayer and I resent any suggestion that taxpayers, civic or provincial, should carry the load for the music lovers.

There are many sections of Vancouver, built up long ago, which are still without sewers. Now sewers may be dull things, but they are important. They may not be "cultural" in the long-hair sense, but they are a sign of high culture, nevertheless, and so necessary!

M. Musspratt

from "Sewers or Symphonies", *The Vancouver Sun*, 6 June 1950.

CBC's "Davie" Dunton will push a button at 6 p.m. Wednesday and Canadian TV will be here....

"It is extremely important for Canada to have a strong system...it could make or break the national sense in the next generation," he said.

from "CBC Chief in City", 15 December 1953, Television Transmitter, Mount Seymour Docket 1, Vancouver City Archives.

During the last 18 months 216 theatres have closed in Canada, 24 of them in B.C. Last week it was announced five more would close in Vancouver. The major reason, say operators, is television.

from "Television Arch Foe of Suburban Movies", *The Vancouver Daily Province*, 15 July 1955.

Top left 1958. CPR cruise ship docks at Pier B-C. Bill Dennett photograph.

Bottom left May 1953. Opening of the Delta Drive-In, Richmond.

18 July 1952. Parade to celebrate the opening of the Arbutus trolley bus service. Forty-first Avenue and Arbutus Street.

Great harm has been done and "unwarranted fears" have been aroused by the unproved theory that polio is transmitted by hens' eggs, according to a Vancouver medical research expert.

from "Hen's Egg Theory on Polio Scored", 14 October 1952, Polio Docket, Vancouver City Archives.

Now that a large proportion of the susceptible population has been innoculated against poliomyelitis it might be profitable to stop and review the situation briefly.

During the years 1945 to 1955, there were a total of 573 cases of poliomyelitis in Vancouver City, with peaks of 139 in 1947, 106 in 1949, 101 in 1952 and 120 in 1953. In 1956, by contrast, there were only 8 cases in Vancouver City and 22 in the whole Metropolitan area. Of these, none died, 12 showed some paralysis and 10 no paralysis. Three of the latter had one or more doses of polio vaccine.

from J.L. Gayton, "Polio and Polio Vaccine", *Public Health Bulletin*, Autumn 1957.

The Federal Government will not make any further contribution to help meet the deficit of the British Empire Games.... The feeling in Ottawa is that Vancouver got a stadium and swimming pool out of the Games and should therefore look after its own deficit.

from Doug Leitermen, "Ottawa Won't Help Meet Big B.E.G. Debt", *The Vancouver Daily Province*, 9 February 1955.

Mr. Knute Buttedahl brought to our attention in *The Sun*, June 26, an ugly incident of racial discrimination at one of our local golf clubs when a Negro contestant was refused the amenities of the club.

It is hoped that no such incident occurs during the progress of the British Empire Games. Vancouver will be host to hundreds of colored peoples from all quarters of the globe. Should racial discrimination be shown by any of our citizens it would be a reflection not only on our hospitality but be a telling blow against Western democracy.

Emma J. Walker,
Chairman, North Shore
Canadian National Refugee Committee

from *The Vancouver Sun*, 10 July 1954.

Top left 1955. Salk vaccination program.

Bottom left 17 June 1958. Collapse of the Second Narrows Bridge. Eighteen workmen and one diver were killed. Gordon Sedawie photograph.

Top 1958. Native children on Musqueam Indian Reserve.

Bottom 7 August 1954. Roger Bannister and John Landy completing "the Miracle Mile" at the British Empire Games, the first time two men had run the mile under four minutes in the same race. Charlie Warner photograph.

NEW LIFE CONFECTIONERY

TOBACCO

MAGAZINES

DRINK
Pepsi-Cola

NEW LIFE JOKE SHOP

活生新

NEW LIFE
CONFECTIONERY
JOKES & NOVELTIES
FOREIGN STAMPS

糖菓雜款

活生新
420

Read Today's Vancouver Sun
MORE to READ in THE PROVINCE

DRINK
KIK
The Family Cola

LIFE
IONERY

STAMPS
LTIES

DRINK
Coca-Cola

An "appalling" housing shortage awaits 5,000 immigrants to be airlifted to Vancouver, say city labor leaders.... The airlift of British, Hungarian and French immigrants begins March 15, but "there's been no planning at all," said Mr. Black [B.C. Federation of Labor president].

from "Immigrants Face Housing Problem", 1 March 1957, Hungarians and Hungary Docket, Vancouver City Archives.

Most British Columbia employees will soon be entitled to two weeks vacation with pay each year. Legislation enforcing this was introduced Monday by Labor Minister Lyle Wicks. It takes effect July 1, 1957, and covers all workers except domestics, farm workers, surveyors and those employed in the professions.

from "New Law to Require 2-Week Vacation", *The Vancouver Sun*, 28 February 1956.

Labor is enraged by the new labor laws because it believes the provincial government is putting the clock back 50 years. Management, on the other hand, believes it is emerging from a dark age in which unions were top-heavy with power....

In brief, Bill 43 wipes out the secondary boycott (refusal to handle "hot" goods); makes information picketing illegal; eliminates the sympathy strike; renders circulation of the "we do not patronize" list unlawful; and makes both unions and employers' organizations legal entities.

It's the legal entities part which hurts labor most. The unions think this will involve them in "endless litigation", give unscrupulous employers the opportunity to drag them into court on the slightest pretext, and make them responsible for what members do even though the leaders may not approve it.

from Doug Collins, "Labor Act Called Return to 1902", *The Vancouver Sun*, 13 March 1959.

Left Storefront on Pender Street. Fred Herzog photograph.

Top ca. 1956. Hornby Street south of the Hotel Vancouver, facing the Court House.

Bottom 1956. Log booms in False Creek.

The sweater girl has done more to improve the posture of modern woman than the whole corset industry, in the opinion of Flora Macdonald, RN, nurse in charge of Burnaby Victorian Order of Nurses.

It's the stance, Miss Macdonald told the Edmonds branch of the VON auxiliary....

from "'Sweater Girl' Improves Posture", *The Vancouver Sun*, 14 October 1954.

"It's a man's world, but the right woman can find a substantial and satisfying place in it." So said Miss Nina Anthony, woman's editor and copy editor of Radio Station CKWX to an interested group of co-eds Tuesday noon....

Jobs available to women include copy writing, layout, selling advertising time and space, buying it, and publicity and public relations work.... Salaries start at about $50 a week.

from "Room for Women in field of Radio", *The Ubyssey*, 27 January 1956.

Read it.
Your life may depend on it.
Why?
You live in a target area. A hydrogen bomb dropped in the area would cause complete destruction for a radius of 4 miles, major damage for a radius of 7 miles, moderate damage for 10 miles.

You must get beyond this 20 mile limit to be reasonably safe.

from *Civil Defense Evacuation and Survival Plan for Greater Vancouver Target Area*, Vancouver City Archives, Pamphlet 1957-28.

This could be the Metro Decade for Vancouver and its surrounding municipalities—linking... [them] in one great organization....

The city will begin to demolish huge areas of blight and slum as part of its 20-year Urban Re-development program....

More suburban shopping "parks" will ease downtown traffic problems—but not entirely or even adequately....

There can only be more Vancouverites in the Sixties, telling more and more Canadians and Torontonians that this is Canada's city of the future.

from "Metro and Grey Cup", *The Vancouver Daily Province*, 2 January 1960.

1959. Car show.

Top left 17 May 1956. Traffic at 5:30 p.m. at Georgia and Granville streets.

Bottom left August 1960. Hastings Street.

May 1971. Demonstration at the
Courthouse fountain on Georgia Street.

In Our Time
1960–1985

The decade of hippies and women's liberation, of environmental and antiwar protests, arrived in Vancouver without a single manifesto or waving flag. But the city was flirting with change: in 1962 citizens voted to allow Sunday movies, and in 1964 to let unescorted women enter bars. In the West End, old homes gave way to highrise apartments, built at the rate of 1,000 suites a year from 1958 to 1971. The growing Port of Vancouver shipped enough grain, lumber and minerals to become, in tonnage, Canada's largest seaport. Fed by new capital, the downtown sprouted shiny head offices and hotels.

But many citizens did not share the developers' dreams for Vancouver, especially when these dreams meant destroying neighbourhoods and landmarks such as the Birks building. Throughout the city, residents began to organize against development. In the late 1960s the Chinese community and its supporters stopped both a proposed freeway through Chinatown and a public housing scheme that had already destroyed part of the Strathcona area. Their success in persuading the federal government to support a locally administered rehabilitation program marked the end of large-scale urban renewal in Canada.

Among the activists in the continuing protests against heavy-handed development was a new group of people distinguished by their long hair, health food diet and taste for soft drugs. Vancouver's hippy population settled in Kitsilano, a neighbourhood of big old houses suitable for communal living. In time the counterculture they represented imposed at least some of its values on the city, in the shape of such organizations as Greenpeace, a worldwide environmental protection group founded in Vancouver. The federal government's Opportunities for Youth and Local Initiatives programs of the mid-1970s sparked an explosion of cultural activity and social services from experimental theatre to legal aid clinics. And in contrast to the struggles of the Vancouver International Festival, which died of red ink in the early 1960s, the Vancouver Children's Festival and the Folk Music Festival sprang into vigorous life.

Growing Chinese, East Indian and Vietnamese communities made their presence felt in new businesses and cultural organizations. Language classes flourished. By 1979, 40 per cent of the city's primary school students spoke English as a second language. Spurred by a planning thrust toward diversity and livability, the inner city blossomed as a "people place." Granville Island and the south shore of False Creek, once the grimy industrial heart of the city, were redeveloped with mixed-income housing and, on the island, theatres, a market and even a brewery.

Vancouver was deeply affected by the recession of the early 1980s. Business bankruptcies and breadlines grew, and housing prices dropped from the speculative highs common at the beginning of the decade. The city pinned its hopes for a revitalized economy on Expo 86, a world transportation and communications exposition that would take place on 200 acres of old CPR land on the north shore of False Creek.

You are, I know, only too well aware of the tremendous growth which has occurred in traffic volumes over the past many years. To give emphasis to this however, it may be worthwhile to recall that only 20 years ago — 1940 — Vancouver had a population of 272,000 and the number of vehicles registered through our Vancouver office was 49,000. That is, we had one vehicle for about every six people living in the city. In 1960, twenty years later ... our population was 410,000 and motor vehicle registration had grown to 166,000 — that is, one vehicle for every 2½ persons. But this is not the most significant statistic.... In that same 20 year period gasoline consumption had a six-fold increase. This means that now we not only have more than three times as many vehicles, but each travels six times more miles than it did 20 years ago.

from Mayor T. Alsbury, in a speech to The Vancouver Traffic & Safety Council, *Annual Report*, 1961, Vancouver City Archives, Pamphlet 1961-126.

Businessmen who think that downtown can only be saved by levelling all the old buildings and raising new ones should consider Robson Street. Here, behind the false fronts and the old fronts of brick and frame buildings dating back 50 years or more, is one of the liveliest shopping sections in town.... Here are foreign restaurants serving new (to Canadians) dishes, small art galleries and print shops, bookstores and jazz record outlets, specialty holes-in-the-wall that sell jewellery and Mexican sombreros and Eskimo carvings and sea shells from all over the south seas....

Robert Fulford, the articles editor of Maclean's said in a recent talk that these scandalously broken-down old storefronts are needed to provide space for small businesses which operate on a modest scale outside the normal stream of commerce. The town planners have no place for these people, he pointed out, but they are essential to the life of a city.

from Frank Walden, "New Canadians Bring New Vitality to Robsonstrasse", *The Vancouver Sun*, 24 August 1963.

1967. The Vancouver Block on Granville Street viewed through an arch of the Burrard Bridge. Dan Scott photograph.

Top left February 1960. Looking west along Nelson Street between Cardero and Bidwell streets.

Bottom left 1960. Looking southeast from Georgia Towers. A solitary B.C. Hydro Building towers over the West End.

It's time we caught up with the times and set to work earnestly to improve the appearance of commercial areas in Vancouver. An ugly hodgepodge of advertising signs, traffic signs and overhead utility wires and poles clutters, defaces and depreciates most of our streets. It is incongruous that such visual squalor should exist in Vancouver, which has one of the most beautiful settings of any city on earth.

from F. W. Ellis, "Remedy for Visual Squalor on Our Streets", in a speech to the Vancouver Board of Trade, 8 November 1962, Vancouver City Archives, Pamphlet 1962-123.

There is no need to recount all the squabble and trauma about Vancouver's courthouse fountain, the provincial government's Centennial gift to the city. In August 1966 alderman Aeneas Bell-Irving summed up most of Vancouver's up-to-here attitude with the comment, "I'm sick of fountains. In Vancouver," he went on, "there is one thing we don't need and that is more fountains, because God has given us a perfectly wonderful supply of rain."

from Eileen Johnson, "A Thing of Beauty, pain in the neck", *The Vancouver Sun*, 1 August 1969.

The giant mop-up goes on. The lower mainland, stunned by the worst storm in memory, is still counting its losses in dead, injured, property damage and worry. Nobody uses the word disaster to describe it, but hurricane-force winds swept through the Greater Vancouver area early Saturday like a monster scythe and left a trail of destruction that staggered the imagination.... Seven persons were killed and scores were injured. Looting broke out in some sections where store windows were smashed.... Thousands dined on cold meats and drinks while huddled in heavy clothing in their homes as they waited for weary Hydro crews to repair downed lines. Anxiety spread for the safety of families and loved ones as telephones, radio and television stations were blacked out by lack of power.... Work crews sweating round the clock succeeded in clearing all the main roadways of fallen trees, but still there is much to be done.

from "Storm-jolted mainland mops up, counts 7 dead, loss in millions", *The Vancouver Province*, 15 October 1962.

September 1960. "Ban the Bomb" protestors at model fallout shelter erected on the Courthouse lawn.

Left 1969. Campbell Avenue docks. Brian Kent photograph.

Vancouver is already a wide-open boom town; now the pressure is on to make it legal.... Vancouver city has licensed 27 cabarets, which are really restaurants in which dancing is permitted. Only five of these are licensed by the provincial government to permit sale of liquor. All the rest serve ice, mixers and glasses, and the patrons serve themselves out of their own liquor bottles. Most of these places run full blast from midnight until 4 a.m. or later; some operate on Sundays.

Chief Constable Booth brought the matter to public attention with a remarkable statement. He said the law is being broken on such a large scale the police have no alternative but to condone much of it. He also said the situation was the city's own fault, but it could be cured by granting more liquor licences.

from Tom Hazlitt, "City's night life roars wide open", *The Vancouver Province*, 9 January 1965.

You've often heard it said that Vancouverites haven't yet got the dining-out habit. But you probably didn't know how Vancouver rates by comparison with other Canadian cities. Well, neither did anyone else until the Dominion Bureau of Statistics released this week a 68-page book compiling its survey of "Urban Family Food Expenditure" in Canada.... Anyway, here is the tabulation of money spent in restaurants per family per week: Montreal, $3.37; Toronto, $2.40; Vancouver, $1.99; Winnipeg, $1.85; Halifax, $1.29; St. John's, Newfoundland, 76 cents.

from "Eat-at-homes", *The Vancouver Sun*, 3 February 1961.

Seldom in Vancouver's entertainment history have so many (20,261) paid so much ($5.25 top price) for so little (27 minutes) as did the audience which screamed at The Beatles in Empire Stadium Saturday night. As music critic I have had to subject my eardrums to more than a little of the cacophony which currently dominates the hit parade but the stuff shouted by these Liverpudlian tonsorial horrors left me particularly unimpressed.

from William Littler, "20,000 Beatlemaniacs Pay So Much — For So Little", *The Vancouver Sun*, 24 August 1964.

Up to October 5th
RONNIE HAWKINS
New Singing Name from Toronto

October 7th to 12th
ERROLL GARNER

October 16th to 26th
EVERLY BROTHERS

Supper show from 7 to 8:30 p.m. includes door charge, top sirloin, prime ribs or salmon steak and dinner show for $5.00 ($6.00 on Fri. and Sat.).

SUPPER CLUB

1136 W. GEORGIA ST.
RESERVATIONS
684-5022 or 683-9827

ca. 1960. Safeway clerks.

Top left 1967. "Robsonstrasse" looking west from Burrard Street.

Bottom left 1966. Oil Can Harry's, 725 Thurlow Street. Dan Scott photograph.

truckin' to Magillas for a

New Years Eve Party

with the COLLECTORS
9pm:4:30am
ECTOPLASMIC ASSAULT LIGHT SHOW & DJANGO
early morning supper
MAGILLAS 759 CARNARVON ST NEW WESTMINSTER

axis
music and bazaar
Sells
LITTLE LUXURIES
at PEOPLE'S PRICES
3752 E. HASTINGS
near Boundary
298-5810
TAKE IN OUR
BLACK-LITE ROOM!

Kind friends recently took some of us old soldiers to the beach for a picnic and I, for one, was startled to behold so many Fidel Castro beards on the men. Why do people harp on the way the girls dress when we have the lordly male making a monkey of himself like this?

Daniel MacLeod
Shaughnessy Hospital

from *The Vancouver Sun*, 12 August 1960.

...Vancouver has the message. Cool it. Vancouver, you see, casual, no-sweat Vancouver, nonchalanting its way through the neurotic 1960s in a pair of Hush Puppies, arrived at its own sweet version of Creative Non-Working long before the rest of us grasped the truth that weekends really *aren't* a worry gap between Friday and whatever's shaking at the office for Monday. Vancouver is Canada's first unwound city....

Its proselytizers, Vancouver natives temporarily strayed from home (they *always* intend to head back one day), are all around, talking it up. Like Allan King, the currently hot movie producer from Vancouver now working out of London, England. "Vancouver's sort of a Lotus Land off behind the hills," he glows. "To me, it's the only beautiful, relaxed, human part of Canada."

from Jack Batten, "Vancouver: Its Message Is: Live!", *Maclean's*, August 1967, Vancouver City Archives, Pamphlet 1967-156.

An American sailor walked head-on into a lamppost but didn't seem to mind. Small boys giggled. Grown men whistled. Elderly women gasped. All of them ... were reacting to Sun reporter Pat Horrobin's attempt to demonstrate the newest London fashion, the thigh-high hemline.

Reporter Horrobin hiked her own hemline six inches above her knees and walked casually among theatre crowds Wednesday to see if there would be any response. There was.... "I've felt more dressed in my polka-dot bikini," she said.

from "Pat's Thigh-High was a Knockout!", *The Vancouver Sun*, 12 August 1965.

The story of sagging brassiere sales in the United States fails to hold up in the Vancouver area. Local lingerie retailers and manufacturers' representatives maintain that most Vancouver women are hooked on bras and are not joining the ban-the-bra movement. In fact, they say, sales are increasing here…. The trend is more apparent among university students and other young people who follow a philosophy of women's liberation. Said a 20-year-old co-ed: "It's one way of being free."

from Lorne Mallin, "Local Girls Not Abreast of Trend", *The Vancouver Sun*, 16 August 1969.

Turning on for the first time? Feeling suicidal? Dissatisfied with your present analyst? Suffering from a bad case of RCMP? Consult Good Trips Incorporated (never a bad trip) Box 120 G. S.

Mount Zion exists. Wanted young men and women, girls and boys who are interested in starting a colony in the mountains of B. C. in the name of love, hope, and charity in preparation for the greater things to come. For information write Box 111 G. S.

JOIN THE DODGE REBELLION
Americans: if you feel the draft, come to warm, safe Canada, the Land of Opportunity. If you are already caught and don't like killing people, by all means DESERT NOW! Don't hesitate. You have nothing to gain but your lives.

from *The Georgia Straight*, classified ads, 24 November 1967.

Vancouver's rats and mice seem to have developed an appetite for grass. Numerous citizens have reported missing stashes. The rodents either steal the bag outright, or chew through the plastic, to devour the grass inside. It is not known what kind of effect this illegal substance has upon them. Concerned citizens have advised us that the best way to deal with this threat is to keep your stash in a glass jar, a tin can, or other rodent-free container.

from *The Georgia Straight*, 8 September 1967.

"Life in the West End is one big sellout." Sue Nasmith, a 24-year-old junior executive with International Business Machines, moved into her high-rise on Jervis five months ago and she's fighting mad. "Everywhere you look you see the would-be swingers arriving on the scene," says the vivacious, brown-eyed brunette....

"I stand on my 15th floor balcony to enjoy my $150 view and I look up to see 50 blank faces peering over their balconies, doing exactly the same thing. I look down into the pool area lined with wall-to-wall bodies — they have paid an extra $25 for the privilege of being there — and no one is speaking to each other.... The farce is this: everybody chooses the West End not because they are swingers but because they want to be, because, in fact they are very lonely people. So they come here, pile up on top of each other, and never say a word."

from Dawn MacDonald, "West End Swingers Aren't Really With It", *The Vancouver Sun,* 19 September 1966.

In the Lower Mainland we have already experienced the pains of park shortage — people turned back from a ski trip, people unable to find enough space at the beach, and people who simply stay at home to avoid being frustrated....

In recent years, the people of the Lower Mainland and their local governments have come to recognize the need for REGIONAL parks as part of our complete park system. This need has arisen, not just as a result of our increased leisure time and increased wealth, but because our social "world" has jumped far beyond the political boundaries of the municipality within which we happen to live.... People are no longer satisfied with only local recreational opportunities and cannot be expected to use only the parks within their municipality.

from "A Regional Parks Plan for the Lower Mainland Region", in a report to The Regional Parks Committee of the Lower Mainland Municipal Association, May 1966.

Top April 1966. An early "paint-in". Fence around Courthouse conceals work being done to install the Centennial Fountain, the province's surprise gift to Vancouver for the 1967 Centennial. George Sedawie photograph.

Bottom May 1966. Lion Dance in Chinatown. Ross Kenward photograph.

Right 1969. Old-timers enjoy pitch and putt at Stanley Park. Ross Kenward photograph.

A radical "seaway" link between the North Shore and downtown Vancouver was put before an interested park board Monday night. The revolutionary plan would, among other things, slash an eight-lane highway through a wild section of Stanley Park, wheel out to sea to form a large salt water lake, and tie in with suggested metro highway systems without hacking through any of the downtown section.

from Bill Dunford, "Freeway over sea planned for city," *The Vancouver Province*, 29 March 1968.

On a dismal morning, October 17, 1967, City Council approved the Carrall Street alignment, a six-block-long, 80-foot-wide elevated freeway link, that would flatten one commercial block of Chinatown, sever the remaining blocks from the city centre and cast a shadow of decay over the area, including Gastown....

By evening of the same day, interested civic groups had united in protest. Students marched in the streets, black mourning banners hung from buildings. A crisis had occurred and a conscience had been awakened. A public meeting overflowed City Council Chambers. This was followed by another public meeting of 1,500 people in an auditorium where 27 groups presented briefs. On January 9, 1968 Council rescinded the Freeway Motion.... Vancouver stopped on the brink of destroying one of its most unique and valuable assets.

from David Nicholas Spearing, "Chinatown: Vancouver's Heritage", *Gastown Gazette*, March 1970, Vancouver City Archives, Pamphlet 1970-122.

There are many reasons why we should re-examine the role of the bicycle in the Kitsilano community. This ingenious machine suitable for commuting or recreation is noted for its lack of noxious exhaust emissions and the relative infrequency with which it knocks down small children and household pets on residential streets....

Unfortunately, cyclists who set out inevitably find the streets are dominated and designed for a heavy opponent (hiss, boo) who is often unwilling to yield a bit of the roadway.

from "Pedal Power!", *around Kitsilano*, September 1973, Vancouver City Archives, Pamphlet 1973-126.

1968. After a decade of development,
few old houses are left among the
highrises of the West End. Dan Scott
photograph.

Remember when HIPPIE meant big in the hips,
And a TRIP involved travel in cars, planes and ships?
When POT was a vessel for cooking things in,
And HOOKED was what Grandmother's rug might have been?...
When lights and not people were SWITCHED ON and OFF,
And the PILL might have been what you took for a cough?...
When FUZZ was a substance that's fluffy like lint,
And BREAD came from bakeries, not from the mint?...
When WAY OUT meant distant and far, far away,
And a man couldn't sue you for calling him GAY?...
Words once so sensible, sober and serious
Are making the FREAK SCENE like PSYCHEDELIRIOUS.
IT'S GROOVY MAN GROOVY, but English it's not.
Methinks that the language has gone straight to POT.

from "Psychedelirium Tremens", *Gastown Gazette*, March 1970, Vancouver City Archives, Pamphlet 1970-122.

A woman in the last month of pregnancy was among those clubbed as police wielded truncheons "indiscriminately" during the fray in Maple Tree Square on Aug. 7, the Gastown inquiry was told Friday.... Mrs. Vivian Palmer, a 27-year-old student at Simon Fraser University, said a policeman with a riot stick hit "an obviously pregnant" woman during the tumult after horses broke up a crowd at a pro-marijuana "smoke-in".... Colin King, a reporter for radio station CKNW said he heard a scream pierce the uproar after the horses moved into the crowd. He saw two policemen drag a blonde girl in hot pants by her hair along Carrall....

Terry Martin, 30, of North Vancouver testified that the horses caused the panic.... The horses galloped along the sidewalks after the initial move through the square. "People were petrified, scattered and falling down."

from Duncan McWhirter, "Pregnant woman hit, probe told", *The Vancouver Province*, 25 September 1971.

1970. Handmade leather goods adorn a Gastown street vendor's cart. Deni Eagland photograph.

Top left September 1973. Ambleside Beach, West Vancouver. Cleaning up the oil spill caused by a collision between the Japanese container ship *Sun Diamond* and the British freighter *Erawan* off Point Grey. Glenn Baglo photograph.

Bottom left June 1970. Vancouver Liberation Front "doing their thing" on the beach during a party at Stanley Park. Glenn Baglo photograph.

ca. 1978. Old homes near Strathcona
School. Fred Herzog photograph.

John Newport is only one — of a few thousand Vancouver senior citizens — who can't get around for some physical or financial reason. But he's convinced he can cope with it. He has his books, his daily newspaper, his radio, and his giant picture window. But what about Mrs. Margie Hamilton who's confined to a wheelchair, or Mrs. Harriet Collingwood who just barely gets around with her walker....

This is exactly why — with the help of an Opportunities for Youth Grant — a group of eight students supplied their own vehicles, quickly installed two-way radios, and set up a transportation service for low-income senior citizens.... After two weeks it was operating at maximum capacity. It is now transporting nearly one hundred people per day.

from Rod Sandlin, "Community Transportation Service", Local Initiatives Application, Vancouver City Archives, Pamphlet 1972-149.

While Wong Young was digging in his vegetable garden one sunny morning this week, a crew of workmen ripped the old and rotted roof off his little East End bungalow. Pensioner Wong, who came here from China 52 years ago, was delighted. He is one of the first people in Canada to benefit from a pioneering urban rehabilitation program that does not involve bulldozing old houses into the ground and replacing them with high-rises.

The Strathcona Rehabilitation Project is refurbishing the neighborhood instead of pulling it down. And the $5 million experiment supported by all three levels of government is the first of its kind in Canada.... The Strathcona story goes back to 1968 when the city announced plans to bulldoze virtually the entire district and erect public housing.

from Moira Farrow, "Old houses torn apart — and rebuilt", *The Vancouver Sun*, 27 May 1972.

Top December 1973. Residents gather at Broadway and Vine to protest traffic deaths. Ralph Bower photograph.

Bottom July 1972. Mount Pleasant residents, 800-block East Broadway. Retta Grayson photograph.

Top 1972. "Hare Krishna" followers in saffron robes chant in front of a downtown department store.

Bottom 1974. Playing for his supper, an old fiddler entertains near a Gastown hotel. Rob Straight photograph.

Elmore and Ray. It sounds like a nightclub act, but Elmore and Ray are really two elder hippies who spend up to 18 hours a day trying — usually with remarkable success — to get runaway teenagers back home and to persuade potential runaways not to leave home.... At first they grandly dubbed their old unpainted house "The Communications Centre," but now it's more simply known as "Cool Aid."

Elmore is Elmore Smalley, 30, who sports the long hair and beads standard for hippies.... Ray is just plain Ray. He won't tell anything more about himself, not even his last name.... Why the secrecy? "We often have to work outside the law," says Elmore, referring to the fact that under the law runaways are supposed to be handled by police or official social service agencies. Yet, says Elmore, "the police don't have as much success as we do with runaways. They take a kid home and leave him there, no questions asked. The kid runs away again within a few days." In contrast, Elmore says he and Ray have succeeded in persuading 170 of the 200 runaways they've talked to since October to go home. And only 20 of those 170 ran away again.

from Stephen Brown, "Runaway teen-agers get some real cool aid", *The Vancouver Province,* 9 March 1968.

The city's newest school — simply called City School — has no principal, no regular classes, no exams, no formal structure of any kind. Since it opened on Sept. 7 the 100 students have decided each morning what they want to do during the day.... Thursday afternoon, for example, about 70 of the pupils studied outdoors in the Little Mountain Park.... A smaller group, on its own, studied the head of a chicken preserved in formaldehyde after the youngsters had cooked and eaten the rest of the chicken.... Another group went to a veterinary hospital and watched an operation on a dog. The children are prolific with the flood of ideas about things they want to see and learn about, the teachers say.

from Wilf Bennett, " 'A little of what you fancy' the byword at new school", *The Vancouver Province,* 17 September 1971.

It is possible to save a user of drugs from a life of horror if detected early. There are not enough doctors in this world to examine each and every suspected drug user, but there are enough parents....

Observe your children for unusual changes in normal behavior. If you suspect your child is using drugs, medical advice should be sought immediately. Any information as to where drugs are being obtained should be forwarded to your local Police Department.

You need not give your name

from *"The Drug Bug"*, pamphlet published by Vancouver Police Department, 1970.

Save the whales, world!!! Your presence is needed at Jericho Park. This site is being used as a departure point for the Greenpeace V boats. After a day of ceremony and celebration, this flotilla will then journey north to Winter Harbour on Vancouver Island's west coast. Once there, the Greenpeace V crew will await this season's whalers, and if all else fails, will place themselves between hunters and prey, and pray. Show your support for these brave ecologists. Spread the news, pack a picnic, bring the tribe, feel the tide, bring a kite, your bike's alright, or catch a whale bus and join us in open appreciation and support.

from "Greenpeace Gathering Jericho Park", advertisement, *The Vancouver Province*, 26 April 1976.

Representatives from Vancouver women's groups, gay groups and children's rights took turns voicing their complaints to Federal Justice Minister Ron Basford following his speech urging implementation of the proposed Human Rights Legislation.... Special interests groups criticized the bill for not providing protection for native women marrying white men, for not dealing with discrimination against homosexuals and for being too wishy-washy about affirmative action programs.

from Joey Thompson, "Making the 'right' promises", *The Vancouver Province*, 2 May 1977.

Top 1978. A game of chance at the Pacific National Exhibition. Fred Herzog photograph.

172

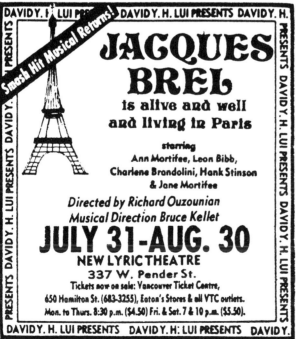

Two dungaree-clad youths were walking across a parking lot at the Habitat Forum, the informal conference paralleling the United Nations Conference on Human Settlement, when a large sedan sped by, enveloping them in a cloud of dust. "That must be one of the delegates from downtown," said one to the other as he shook off the dust.

The incident underscored the differences between the forum, as the informal conference is known, and "downtown," the official meeting, known as Habitat.... The main conference is dealing largely with political matters as it struggles toward agreement on a final version of a set of guidelines for international action on housing and urban issues.... The Forum, housed at Jericho Beach ... is a casual, confused amalgam of meetings, seminars and exhibits, with almost as much space given to ethnic food stands as to meeting rooms.

from Paul Goldberger, "Youthful Forum That Parallels the Habitat Conference is Virtually Another World", *The New York Times*, 9 June 1976.

"If you want someone to credit for the fact that this has become a great restaurant town, you can thank the federal government's immigration policy" [says Alex MacGillivray, long-time restaurant critic]. Besides the European bistro explosion, there are some 200 Chinese restaurants in the Vancouver area, some of which many consider superior to those in San Francisco. There is a plethora of breezy Greek restaurants spearheaded by burly, bearded Aristedes Pasparakis, 36, whose sprawling Orestes on West Broadway legitimized Greek food and dining when it opened more than five years ago, spawning some 45 imitators on the Lower Mainland.... Other more traditional top-line restaurants ... have also combined to tempt Vancouverites to spend almost twice as much in restaurants (15.6 per cent of disposable income as opposed to 9.4 per cent) as their Eastern brethren.

from Thomas Hopkins, "A whole new dimension to Western hospitality", *Maclean's*, 1 January 1979.

173

It is the most talked about trial held here in years. Everyone in Vancouver, it seems, knew about the Penthouse cabaret, a family-run business that hadn't been closed since it opened in the late 1940s as a private residence with guests making a minimum contribution of $1.75 to the Eagle-Time Athletic Club. But the club has been closed since Dec. 24, 1975, when police raided the Penthouse, carrying off six cardboard cartons of records over six hours while topless dancers kept on performing on stage. Now, the owners and management of the Penthouse have been charged with conspiring with other persons to live on the avails of prostitution and conspiring to corrupt public morals.

from Malcolm Gray, "The big Vancouver 'charge-sex trial' ", *The Globe and Mail*, 24 September 1976.

Beginning June 17th, the new Sea-Bus service really goes to town. All that bumper-to-bumper bridge hassle can be a thing of the past. Avoid the rush hour crunch and sail across Burrard Inlet like a breeze ... in a matter of minutes. And with fast, frequent bus connections at Lonsdale Quay and Granville Waterfront Station you can go transit all the way.

from "How to win at the game of bridge", Province of British Columbia Ministry of Municipal Affairs and Housing advertisement, 8 June 1977, Vancouver City Archives, Pamphlet 1977-9.

Folk hero and former astronaut Neil Armstrong, the first man to set foot on the lunar surface on Sunday, July 20, 1969, at 7:56 p.m. (Vancouver time) — was the first to officially enter the Harbour House restaurant and observation deck atop the Harbour Centre complex at 555 West Hastings Street. Ceremonies were held at 10:01 a.m. — eight years, 22 days, 14 hours and five minutes after Armstrong placed his left boot on the moon.... Armstrong, now 52 ... placed the same foot (Gucci Loafer size 9½ B) on a flat of fresh cement atop the Harbour Centre to leave the imprint of his famous step in Vancouver.

from "One Sticky Step by Neil; Harbour House Opens!", *The Observer, Harbour House Restaurant and Observation Deck*, 1983.

Top 1981. 1000-block East Broadway, slated for demolition and apartment redevelopment. Rick Loughran photograph.

Bottom 5 July 1981. An explosive end to the Devonshire Hotel.

Sir — Every time I traverse the Granville Mall I am frustrated and indignant. How can the $3.2 million spent on its construction be justified? It is hardly different from the original street. It is now curved instead of straight, the sidewalks have been widened 25 feet, the shapes of the lighting standards have been altered and some trees have been planted.

There was a short period before the mall was officially opened when it was pleasant to stroll along its sidewalks. The buses were still using the temporary routes assigned them during construction.... One could even visualize that despite the dreadful dark towers and Eaton's ghastly architecture, the mall might yet become a pleasant people place. Now however, at peak periods of the day there are over 50 buses lumbering up and down Granville. It is just any old big city street.

(Ms.) C. Bloomfield

from *The Vancouver Sun*, 10 April 1975.

Back in the late sixties I moved my graphics and design studio into the just-rediscovered Gastown area. The people who were renting the old buildings were mostly young craftspeople, artists and artisans of varying degrees of ability, enthusiasm and business sense. There was a strong sense of community and most of the people who operated the little shops lived in or close to Gastown....

People came to see and feel the 'bohemian' atmosphere, the sense of freedom from conventionality, the funky stores with *low-priced*, handcrafted products, and the weird people.... Since activity means business, commercialism started to flourish in Gastown. Some of it came from the 'hippies' themselves whose craft stores flourished and the rest came from the 'uptown' businessmen who realized there was a goldrush in the making. As business boomed, rents and building prices increased rapidly and so did taxes. Only the efficient profit-oriented businesses could afford to stay and reap the rewards, the marginal ones had to leave.

from "Island attracts craftsmen", *Granville Island News*, January 1978.

May 1977. Looking north across the
new residential community of False
Creek.

Top November 1983. Solidarity supporters march around the provincial government complex on Hornby Street to protest government cutbacks. Bev Davies photograph.

Bottom October 1978. Hundreds of spectators fill Robson Square during its official opening. Colin Price photograph.

Hearing of the flight of Vietnamese people from their homeland, many Canadians have shown a desire to help, but without having any knowledge of the refugees themselves.... It is becoming increasingly clear that there is a need to provide some information about these people so that the sensitive task of introducing them to their new country can be undertaken with understanding....

Most Vietnamese are not as gregarious or extroverted as the average Canadian, therefore: Talk quietly in a low voice. A loud voice and/or gesture will be interpreted as displeasure. Don't expect them to discuss their problems, concerns, or feelings immediately. Even after the language barrier is cracked, the Vietnamese family is quite autonomous and fiercely independent. The family is the arena for such discussions and only if there is no solution will an outsider be consulted.... Explain what you want them to do then watch to see that they have interpreted your directions correctly. Their smile does not mean they understand, nor does their 'yes'. Don't be misled if they don't look you in the eye. To do so would be immodest and not humble.

from Ed Martin, "Background paper on the Vietnamese Refugees", City of Vancouver, 4 September 1979.

The dust precipitates gracefully through a window on to the nose of a regal lion guarding the old provincial courthouse on Georgia Street. You're thankful stone can't sneeze. The dust is being raised by 70 workers churning old brick and plaster walls into powder and stiffening the structure with concrete as they fashion the courthouse into the Vancouver Art Gallery's new home.

When it opens — fall, 1983, is the target for a first exhibition — $16.8 million [ultimately $20.5 million] will have been spent to refurbish Francis Rattenbury's 1912 heritage building. The VAG's present home on Georgia occupies 42,000 square feet, 12,000 for public galleries. The courthouse complex will have 164,000 square feet, 48,000 alone for exhibition space.

from "Stately home for art gallery", *The Vancouver Sun*, 22 April 1982.

Sitting in the back of the bus that was to transport the Whitecaps to a tumultuous Sunday afternoon welcome downtown, forward Trevor Whymark popped a pen into his mouth and was about to sign an autograph with his cigarette. He stopped for a second and shook his head. Scoring the team's two goals Saturday, a sleepless night of celebration in New York City, jet lag and now this — 1,500 cheering soccer fans welcoming the team at the airport....

Older Vancouverites said the welcome given Vancouver's first professional championship team since the B.C. Lions won the Grey Cup in 1964 far surpassed anything this city has ever seen.... About 50,000 people were downtown to welcome their team home.

from Edie Austin, "Vancouver blows its top giving a wild welcome to victorious Whitecaps", *The Vancouver Sun*, 10 September 1979.

Vancouver's homosexual community will host its own scaled-down version of the Summer Olympics this week. Athletes from four U.S. cities and several provinces will compete in nine events from Thursday to Monday in the 1984 Vancouver Gay Summer Games.... The games, to be held at several locations, will lead into Gay Pride Week, which will start with a parade starting at Nelson and Thurlow at 11 a.m. Monday.

from "Gays to compete", *The Vancouver Sun*, 1 August 1984.

With the massive turnout for Saturday's protest march to buoy them, Solidarity leaders have given themselves two weeks to avert a confrontation they say could lead to a general strike. The sentiment for a general strike was widely in evidence among the estimated 50,000 to 65,000 protesters who marched past the Hotel Vancouver, where the Social Credit party was holdings its annual convention.... The turnout was Solidarity's largest ever, and the second biggest in Vancouver history, topped only by last spring's peace march of 65,000.

from Bob Sarti, "Solidarity sets deadline", *The Vancouver Sun*, 17 October 1983.

1982. Antinuclear rally at Sunset Beach. David Jacklin photograph.

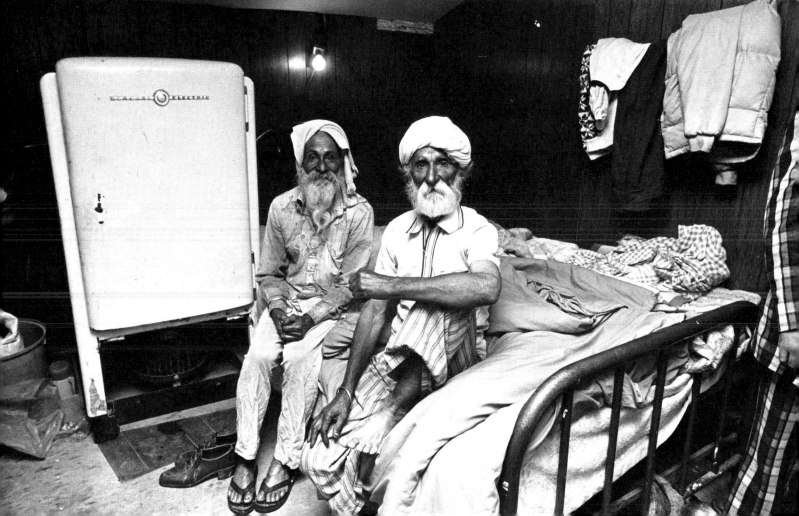

"One! Two! Three! Four!" On the floor of
Terpsichore, a Vancouver dance studio,
three dozen young women dressed in
leotards are scissoring the air with their
legs. Rock 'n' roll music thumps.... It's the
latest wrinkle in the fitness craze, a mixed
bag of dance and calisthenics known as
"dancercise," "jazz exercise" or "aerobic
dance." But whatever they call it,
thousands of women and some men are
now "taking from" someone, as the jargon
would have it, huffing and puffing two or
three times a week through hour-long
sequences of muscle manipulation.
Storefront dancercise studios have sprung
up like fast-food outlets. In one three-block
downtown Vancouver area, 12 have
blossomed recently.

from John Faustmann, "Shaking a leg for fitness",
Maclean's, 23 March 1981.

Racism is a part of life for most East
Indians, said Charan Gill, chairman of the
B.C. Organization to Fight Racism.
Whether it is felt through violence and
hurled insults, or more subtle forms such
as jokes and stereotyping, Gill said racism
is something with which East Indians
must always be prepared to deal: "We seem
to be last on the list. It used to be the
Chinese and the Italians."

from Shelley Banks, "Racism is 'part of our life' ",
The Vancouver Sun, 7 January 1981.

A Lower Mainland rental vacancy rate,
which some say is now "below zero," may
force people to live in tents and cars by the
summer.... "The (provincial government's)
emergency shelters are full and we're
putting so many people into motels that
we're getting discount rates," says Linda
Mead of the non-profit Red Door
Society.... "It's particularly hard on
families, especially if there are a lot of
children because as rents go up so does
discrimination against children...."

In its latest quarterly housing outlook,
CMHC says housing construction is in its
worst slump since the Depression. Starts on
new housing units will decline in 1980 for
the fourth consecutive year, the longest
decline since one that ended in 1933.

from Chuck Poulsen, "Vancouver rent crisis may put
families in tents", *The Vancouver Province*, 17 February
1980.

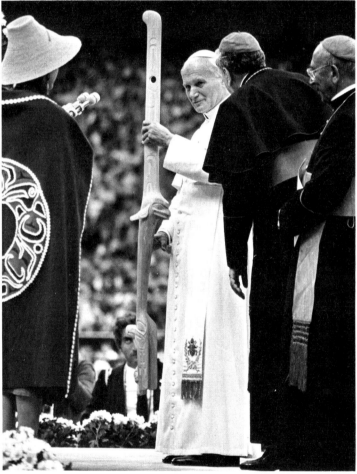

18 September 1984. Pope John Paul
II receives a "talking stick" in a
ceremony at B.C. Place Stadium. Ian
Lindsay photograph.

Top left January 1985. Granville Island
Public Market is the heart of the
Granville Island development, whose
shops, restaurants and cultural facilities
attract thousands of visitors daily.
Henri Robideau photograph.

Bottom left 1981. Fraser Valley
farmworkers. Steve Bosch photograph.

Hidden by cliffs at the foot of the Point Grey headland, Vancouver's Wreck Beach was once the preserve of the daring and eccentric few, but no more. Today doctors and lawyers, as well as university students, airline attendants and Moroccan-dark backpackers from Quebec, clamber down its 60-metre bluffs, all eager to indulge in a little au naturel sunbathing on the country's most famous nude beach....

Officially, Wreck Beach does not exist. For years its isolation and the relatively small crowds using it kept the "problem" in the closet. In the late '60s as the beach became increasingly popular, city officials were presented with something of a fait accompli.

from John Masters, "Bare encounters with the sun-worshipping set", *Maclean's*, 31 August 1981.

Federal tax collectors want to take a $100 million bite out of the $200 million in profits earned by Greater Vancouver "flippers" who bought and resold homes during the 1980-81 real estate boom.... The tax department classifies a flip as a sale of property bought for speculation and sold again within 12 months....

"We estimate the speculators in Greater Vancouver earned up to $200 million during the boom," Revenue Canada-Taxation spokesman Ina McMillan said Tuesday.... The boom began in July of 1980, when the average house sold through the Real Estate Board of Greater Vancouver for $109,600 and rose at the rate of $5,000 a week to an average of $181,200 by April 1981.

from Brian Power, "Taxman chases house 'flips' ", *The Vancouver Sun*, 5 May 1982.

Pharmacist Art Chin isn't too happy about the prescription for his rapid-transit problems. B.C. Transit plans to dig two huge holes in the new Shopper's Drug Mart store at 2606 Commercial Drive and insert pylons to carry the ALRT's elevated tracks.... Trains will whoosh overhead every three minutes but Chin says: "I was kind of relieved, because at the beginning they (B.C. Transit) were talking about expropriating everyone in sight."

from "Druggist swallows bitter transit pill", *The Vancouver Province*, 14 August 1983.

Top 1984. Vancouver Children's Festival at Vanier Park. John S. Edgar photograph.

Bottom July 1980. Vancouver Folk Music Festival at Jericho Beach. Steve Bosch photograph.

Left 1984. Two members of Negavision at "Apocalypso", a punk rock event held in a warehouse. David Jacklin photograph.

Gateway to the Pacific 1985–1990

Vancouver's centennial brochures heralded 1986 as "The Best Party in 100 Years!" In preparation, Lion's Gate Bridge was festooned with lights, colourful banners were flown along the new Cambie Street Bridge, and the spectacular sails of the new Canada Place Trade and Convention Centre were raised. On the eve of its 100th birthday, Vancouver built a new train for the second century: a light rapid transit system called SkyTrain.

With its sights set on becoming "a world-class city," Vancouver invited the world to Expo 86. Millions accepted the invitation. To make room for the deluge of tourists, an estimated 1,000 long-time residents of downtown eastside rooming hotels were evicted. Many Vancouverites boycotted the fair in protest. For those who could afford it, Expo brought an eclectic range of events including the Kirov Ballet and the world's largest hockey stick, the treasures of Ramses II and a mascot named Ernie, a pop-singing robot. It left behind Science World and a $349 million debt.

After Expo, the pace of change in Vancouver accelerated dramatically — some said alarmingly. The 1930s slogan "Gateway to the Pacific" became a reality; Vancouver confirmed its role as a hub of Pacific Rim trade, largely through intense efforts to court Asian investors.

By 1989, an estimated 4,000 people were moving to Vancouver each month from across the country and across the ocean. Although fewer Asian newcomers than Canadians migrated to Vancouver post-Expo, they more visibly changed the city. While pillars of the establishment called for tighter controls on immigration and investment from Asia, city hall and multicultural organizations tried to defuse the backlash through race relations education.

Construction began on the city's biggest-ever developments: the $2 billion Pacific Place megaproject on the Expo lands, and Marathon Realty's massive Coal Harbour project on the downtown waterfront. At the same time, demolition of the Georgia Medical-Dental building and other historic landmarks sparked greater concern for heritage preservation. Throughout the city, bungalows and three-storey walk-ups fell to the wrecker's ball, and rental vacancies hovered near zero. Angry at city hall and developers alike, residents formed neighbourhood lobby groups.

Meanwhile, more people were homeless, compelled to sleep under bridges and in doorways. Increased economic disparity produced unsettling contrasts: food bank line-ups grew longer while posh new restaurants served $600 soup.

Established arts organizations struggled to survive, but new cultural events — First Night, the Fringe, the writers', jazz, comedy and film festivals — flourished. The movie industry discovered the city, and Vancouverites began to see familiar streets and landmarks in the latest Hollywood hits.

Commercial Drive replaced Fourth Avenue as the centre of the city's thriving counterculture. With the growing numbers of political exiles from El Salvador and Guatemala, Spanish was added to the spoken rhythms of street life on "the Drive."

As awareness of the global ecological crisis grew, Vancouverites embraced the environmental movement. Six thousand participated in the first Mayor's Walk for the Environment in 1989, and citizens welcomed the municipal Blue Box recycling program launched in 1990. A popular bumper sticker read: "Think Globally, Act Locally."

The ripple effect of the Expo extravaganza, which will see 1.5 million more visitors to Vancouver than in a normal summer, is starting to spread through the economy.... "Quite a few customers have said they are getting ready for guests," said Doreen Kong of the staples department of The Bay downtown. "It's not only sheets and pillows. Towels are also selling well...." In Richmond, Ikea store manager Steen Kanter ... [says] "Kitchens are going extremely well because mother-in-law is coming for Expo...." Sofa beds, presumably for those out-of-town guests, are a particularly hot item, he added.
from Alan Daniels, "Love Affair: Firms express great expectations as they court Expo patron's dollar", *The Vancouver Sun*, 1 February 1986.

"It was Black Monday...." Downtown Eastside Residents Association organizer Jim Green had been saying for months that the old and disabled would be evicted in large numbers from hotels and rooming houses to make way for Expo 86 tourists. Today DERA is trying to help find new lodgings for up to 100 people in two hotels who were given eviction notices last weekend.... The DERA survey indicated that at least 30 hotels in the downtown east side are planning renovations that could result in displacement of more than 1,000 residents, despite promises from the B.C. Hotels Association that long-term residents would not be evicted.
from Robert Sarti, "Expo blamed as 2 hotels evict elderly and disabled", *The Vancouver Sun*, 25 February 1986.

A metropolis of 1.3m people, of innumerable nationalities, [Vancouver] still has the public manners of an English country town half a century ago. It seldom raises its voice. It would not dream of jumping a light.... Quiet, frequent, meticulously driven are the buses. Sleek and smooth is the SkyTrain.... Majestically accelerates the catamaran SeaBus across the Burrard Inlet. There are taxis especially humped to accommodate wheelchairs in Vancouver, and talking elevators for the blind, and the aerial tramway that runs up to the summit of Grouse Mountain every day is operated by brisk, well-exercised girls of unimaginable helpfulness.
from Jan Morris, "Have A Nice Day", *Saturday Night*, February 1988.

Vancouver, barely past its 100th birthday, is going to become an Asian city.... What lies in Vancouver's tomorrow is not just immigration, but migration — a phenomenal historic movement of people from one side of the Pacific to the other, as phenomenal as the movement of Europeans across the Atlantic to North America's other coast. In a measure, it is masked by the fact that people from the rest of Canada still account for most of Vancouver's net in-migration.... It is the other indicators that are more significant.... Look at the urban densities on the Asian side of the Pacific Rim and compare them with Vancouver's. Look at the ease and cheapness of world travel, the ubiquitous electronic links of world business, the splendid livability of Vancouver.

from Michael Valpy, "Face of Vancouver to be radically altered", *The Globe and Mail*, 20 February 1989.

Nelson Tsui only had to visit Vancouver once to know this would be home.... Tsui felt Vancouver offered him and his wife Patricia Haley-Tsui the best opportunity to have their cross-cultural marriage blend into the social landscape. "One of the things that struck me was the number of mixed couples," Nelson Tsui said. "In Vancouver you really don't see people staring at you from across the street. It is much more accepted. That is really one of the major reasons for moving to Vancouver for me," he said.... About 30 per cent of Vancouver's population are visible minorities, the highest percentage in Canada.

from Kevin Griffin, "A place of acceptance for inter-cultural romance", *The Vancouver Sun*, 24 October 1989.

Vancouver has outdone every city with its Flame of Peace Monument, located at the south end of the Burrard Street bridge. This newest addition to the city's urban landscape may be the world's most perfectly formed ugly sculpture.... Rising from a truncated pyramid, topped with a Mr. Potato Head boulder, sits a concrete slab on which the eternal flame is to burn. Look on this work and despair.

from Oraf, "Potato Head Inflammatory", *The Georgia Straight*, 21 August 1987.

Page 182 October 1986. Expo 86 featured pavilions from more than 80 nations, provinces, states and corporations. Gerry Kahrmann photograph.

Left 2 May 1986. The monorail glides over opening day crowds at Expo 86. Greg Osadchuk photograph.

Top 13 August 1986. The False Creek Racing Canoe Club wins the first annual Dragon Boat races on False Creek. Peter Battistoni photograph.

Bottom August 1986. Teens on Granville Mall. Mark Van Manen photograph.

Top 1987. The Galleria II condominium development in Fairview Slopes is typical of the last stage of redevelopment of one of Vancouver's oldest neighbourhoods. Bill Keay photograph.

Bottom 1986. All over the city, new mini-malls like this one at Broadway and Alma began to compete with the traditional corner store. David Clark photograph.

The route to Diddly Squat has bright posters that warn: "Developers Keep Out." But the 15-odd squatters occupying a row of modest bungalows in Vancouver's East End have little hope that the posters, or anything else they might try, will stave off imminent eviction by a condominium developer.... The formation of the squatters alliance ... is the latest twist in a housing squeeze which ... saw 1,009 affordable rental units demolished for 816 luxury suites in the first seven months of last year.... Noreen Shanahan, a spokes-woman for the Tenants Rights Coalition, said squatting is bound to increase as the shortage of rental accommodation contin-ues and as decent housing is emptied and demolished to make way for condominiums.
from Deborah Wilson, " 'Thou shalt not pay rent' is Diddly Squat occupants' creed", *The Globe and Mail*, 18 April 1990.

Home builders are listening to the demands of young urban professionals.... New devel-opments like the St. Moritz in Vancouver's tony Kerrisdale district provide what a luxury unit should: lobby surrounded by water garden; Mediterranean-designed swimming pool; gas fireplace with marble hearth; built-in vacuum; custom carpet; Italian brass hardware; Sub-Zero fridge; microwave, and more in 1,100 to 2,500 sq. ft. for $235,000 to $625,000.
from "Wanted: bright, compact, automated for gourmet bathers", *Vancouver Magazine*, April 1987.

If you have had the misfortune to look around the city of Vancouver lately, you cannot help but notice the proliferation of the colour pink.... The first significant example of this style to hit Vancouver was the Terry Fox Memorial in front of B.C. Place. Its effect on the city of Vancouver has been immense. We now have a pink sky-scraper, Park Place, and a rusty pink one, the Bank of B.C. We have a whole street that should be renamed Pinkstrasse, with the glitzy Robson Fashion Park soon to be followed by the first pink White Spot. There is even a new ring of pink neon around the top of the Blue Horizon.
from Oraf, "Pinkification Takes Over", *The Georgia Straight*, 20 February 1987.

Six-year-old Mitchell Linares peeks inside the silver foil bag like he's opening a Christmas present. Ham and egg on a sourdough roll. While the cafeteria tables fill up around him, Mitchell steadily works his way through the sandwich, some soup, containers of juice and a plum. "Can I have another juice?" he asks by 12:05. It's the fourth day of Seymour elementary school's new lunch program, part of the Vancouver school district's attempt this year to find a new way of feeding children who come to school hungry.... Unlike some other school cafeterias, there are no food fights, and very little food thrown in the garbage.

from Frances Bula, "School lunch program wins kids' lip-smacking approval", *The Vancouver Sun*, 19 September 1988.

Seventy anti-abortion protesters were arrested and are to be charged with mischief after they blocked the entrance to Vancouver's abortion clinic for more than six hours Thursday.... When the entrance was cleared after 2 p.m., several women, hiding their faces with scarves and purses, were escorted inside by clinic volunteers.... After the arrests, an official ... acknowledged for the first time that abortions now are being performed in the Everywoman's Health Clinic on 44th at Victoria Drive. Joy Thompson ... said no amount of demonstrating will force the clinic to close.... "They will not stop us. It will not alter our plans. We're operating a medical facility that is legal, and women have a right to this service."

from William Boei, "Abortion protesters face charges after 70 hauled away from clinic", *The Vancouver Sun*, 16 December 1988.

Editor,
During the recent controversy over the demolition of the Georgia Medical-Dental Building, it was often compared to the Marine Building, which was held up as the best example of the Art Deco style in Canada, and a sacrosanct landmark.... Citizens of Vancouver are increasingly alarmed about the rapid destruction of our heritage. Losing the floor of the Marine Building is symptomatic of a greater problem, one we all must address.
Valda Vidners

from *The West Ender*, 18 May 1989.

Top March 1989. House on south Granville Street. For sale: $2.5 million. Ian Smith photograph.

Bottom October 1989. At home underneath the SkyTrain tracks. Jon Murray photograph.

189

There are many individuals at this very gathering who recall vividly ... the terror and the disbelief as they were stripped of citizenship rights, herded together and branded "enemy alien," dispossessed and forced to undergo the breakup of family and community.... I hope that the memory of Japanese Canadian internment, made public on this PNE plaque, will contribute, in some small or large way, toward our common struggle to create a society where racism is checked by mutual understanding and the constant vigilance of us all. Redress was the dream of "justice in our time." It was a desire to transform the pain of internment into an affirmation of citizenship rights.

from Dr. Roy Miki, "Unveiling the Historic Plaque", *The Japanese Canadian Citizens Association Bulletin*, April 1989.

Real Men don't buy kids. More than 300 children under 18 were bought for sex in Vancouver this year. This is not prostitution. This is child sexual abuse.

from a Family Services of Greater Vancouver public education campaign, 1988.

Vancouver's intravenous drug users will get free needles starting Feb. 27 through the city's needle exchange program aimed at stopping the spread of AIDS.... The program ... will distribute 10,000 needles a month to illicit drug users in the downtown area through a storefront centre run by the Downtown Eastside Youth Activities Society.... Although Vancouver is not the first Canadian city to start a needle exchange program, it does have one of the highest counts of AIDS victims in the country ... and the city has already encountered its first case of a baby contracting the fatal disease.

from Jeff Lee, "Drug users to get free needles Feb. 27", *The Vancouver Sun*, 8 February 1989.

Residents eager to use the city's Blue Box recycling program are just that — too eager.... Now the city is coming up with more educational material to teach Blue Box users how to cope with the system. The only materials that can be collected are cans, newspaper, glass and rigid plastics.... The city hopes to cover all of Vancouver by the end of summer.

from Tom Zillich, "Blue Box users too eager", *The East Ender*, 19 July 1990.

Top left December 1987. Working on a winter project. Greg Osadchuk photograph.

Bottom left May 1987. Vancouverites at an annual candlelight vigil for friends and loved ones who died of AIDS. By 1990, Aquired Immune Deficiency Syndrome had claimed the lives of more than 400 local people; about 300 more were battling the disease. Ian Smith photograph.

Top June 1988. Students and supporters protest the closure of School Canadiana, which offered English as a Second Language classes to adults and children in the Strathcona neighbourhood. Steve Bosch photograph.

Right 1987. Over a three-and-one-half year run, *No' Xya'* toured throughout B.C., across Canada and into traditional Maori communities in New Zealand. Ken N. Mowat, artist.

HEADLINES THEATRE & GITKSAN-WET'SUWET'EN TRIBAL COUNCIL
PRESENT THE NATIONAL TOUR OF

NO' XYA'
(OUR FOOTPRINTS)
A PLAY ABOUT SELF-GOVERNMENT

The persistent reputation of this city's securities market as a purveyor of investor rip-offs forced the government to give the regulators the resources to try to clean it up. Since 1987 the strengthened superintendent of brokers office has been trying to make Howe Street look more like Wall Street.... Down on Howe Street they think boards of directors are necessarily different here in the Wild West. Company directors are nearly always insiders — executives and family members. They look after themselves, but no one looks out for the small shareholder. Formalities like board meetings are often dispensed with in this fast-paced market. But that's no longer acceptable for a city being groomed as an international financial centre.

from Judy Lindsay, "Scam capital New York, not Vancouver, Pezim says", *The Vancouver Sun*, 11 September 1990.

The death of a track worker in the final hours of Vancouver's three-day Molson Indy event cast a pall over the success of the racing, which drew the highest attendance of any car race in Canadian history.

from Harold Munro, "Death mars Indy race success", *The Vancouver Sun*, 4 September 1990.

They are the couriers, the spirited young bearers of invoices and blueprints whose vision of the city is one of canyons and forests, their Walkmans permanently tuned into Radio Free Ansel Adams. Me and my bike; my bike and me. Cybernetic fusions of flesh, tubular titanium, Spandex, Velcro and cellular technology. Underneath their mirrored glasses they are headed somewhere that transcends the Bentall Centre with a one-hour rush delivery.

from Doug Coupland, "Straight off the street", *Vancouver Magazine*, August 1987.

Top December 1988. Vancouverites protested that all suites in the Regatta condominium development in Fairview were sold to nonresidents before construction was completed.

Bottom July 1989. Kerrisdale seniors protest demolition of an apartment building at 43rd Avenue and Balsam. Brian Kent photograph.

Right March 1990. SkyBridge to the new Scott Road station. The light rapid transit route was extended to 24.5 km, cutting commuting time between Surrey and downtown Vancouver from about one hour by car to 31 minutes on the SkyTrain. Colin Price photograph.

Critics gave the Pacific Place megaproject a rough ride last night at the Plaza 500. An overflow crowd packed a public hearing to jeer and cheer the 7,650-home development proposed for the former Expo lands on False Creek in Vancouver.... But Concord Pacific spokesman Stanley Kwok said the development exceeded the city's objectives. "We believe your approval will allow us to create tomorrow's heritage."

from Ian Austin, "Megaproject attacked", *The Vancouver Province*, 3 November 1989.

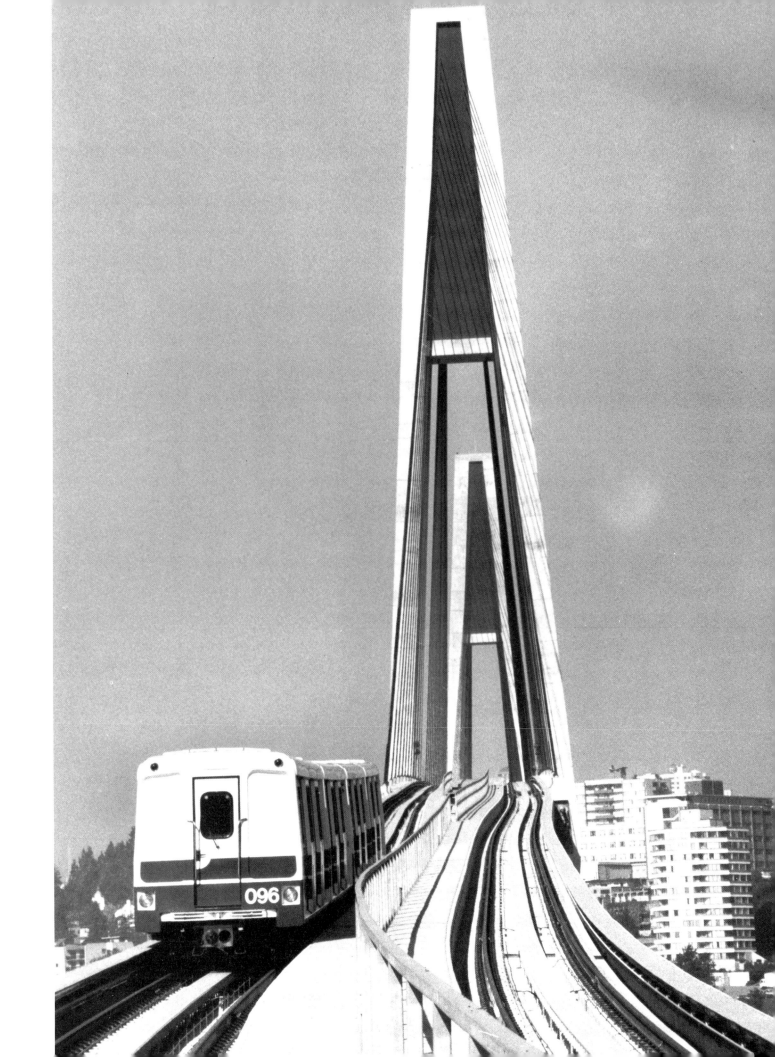

Acknowledgements

We acknowledge the courtesy of the following individuals and institutions in supplying photographs:

Bill Cunningham: p. 138
Bev Davies: p. 176(top)
J. S. Edgar: p. 181 (top)
Fred Herzog: pp. 132, 148, 168, 171
David Jacklin: pp. 177, 180
Kitsilano High School: p. 142 (bottom)
Jack Lindsay: pp. 122 (bottom), 128 (top, bottom), 129, 131, 134, 135, 136 (top), 137
New Westminster Public Library: p. 7 (bottom)
Notman Photographic Archives, McCord Museum: pp. 2, 22, 44
British Columbia Archives and Records Service: pp. 4 (top), 37 (top), 53 (top), 64 (bottom), 70
Public Archives of Canada: p. 59
Henri Robideau: pp. 178 (top)
Vancouver City Archives: pp. 5, 6, 8 (top, centre, bottom), 9, 10-11, 13 (top), 14, 15 (top, bottom), 16 (bottom), 18, 19 (top, bottom), 24, 25 (top, bottom), 26 (bottom), 29 (top), 30, 31 (centre, bottom), 32-3, 34 (top, bottom), 36 (bottom), 37 (top, bottom), 40, 41 (top, bottom), 42 (top, bottom), 44 (bottom), 45, 46, 47 (top, bottom), 50 (bottom), 53 (bottom), 54, 56, 62 (top, bottom), 64 (top), 65 (top, bottom), 68-9, 71 (top), 72 (bottom), 73 (bottom), 74, 76, 79 (centre, bottom), 80 (bottom), 81 (bottom), 82 (top, bottom), 86, 87 (bottom), 92, 93 (bottom), 94 (top), 97, 98, 103, 104 (bottom), 106 (top), 108 (top, bottom), 109, 110-11, 115, 120, 122 (top), 145, 149 (top), 154 (top)
The Vancouver Province: pp. 94, 139 (top), 152, 157, 158 (top), 163, 174 (top), 176 (bottom), 182, 184, 186 (bottom), 187 (bottom), 188 (top), 191
Vancouver Public Library: pp. 4 (bottom), 7 (top), 13 (bottom), 16 (top), 17, 26 (top), 28, 29 (bottom), 31 (top), 35 (top, bottom), 44 (top), 50 (top), 51 (top, bottom), 55 (top), 57 (top), 63, 66, 67 (top, bottom), 71 (bottom), 72 (top), 73 (top), 75, 80 (top), 81 (top), 83, 84, 87 (top), 88 (top, bottom), 89, 93 (top, centre), 95, 96 (top, bottom), 99 (top, bottom), 100, 102 (top, bottom), 104 (top), 105 (top, bottom), 106 (bottom), 114, 115 (top), 116 (top, bottom), 117, 118, 124 (top, bottom), 125 (top, bottom), 130, 142 (top), 144 (bottom), 146 (top, bottom), 147 (top), 150 (top, bottom), 151, 154 (bottom), 159, 162 (top, bottom), 169 (bottom), 170 (top)

The Vancouver Sun: pp. 139 (bottom), 144 (top), 147 (bottom), 149 (bottom), 155, 156, 158 (bottom), 165, 166 (top, bottom), 167, 169 (top), 170 (bottom), 174 (bottom), 175, 178 (bottom), 181 (bottom), 185 (top, bottom), 186 (top), 187 (top), 188 (bottom), 189 (top), 190 (top, bottom)

Map of Vancouver, 1890, courtesy of Vancouver City Archives

Advertisements used courtesy of the following:

American Airlines, p. 116, American Airlines
Best Foods, p. 127, The Canadian Starch Company Limited, Best Foods division
Bolo Billy, p. 117, Hudson's Bay Company
B.C. Electric, pp. 90, 103, 142, B.C. Hydro and Power Authority
B.C. Tel, p. 164, British Columbia Telephone Company
Chevrolet, p. 140, General Motors of Canada Limited
Cypress Spa Tubs, p. 173, Cypress Home Recreation Centre Limited
Jiffy, p. 141, General Foods Limited
Magillas, p. 160, Bob Masse
No' Xya', p. 189, Gitksan & Wet'suwet'en Hereditary Chiefs and Headlines Theatre
Orange Crush, p. 107, reproduced with the permission of Crush International Limited, Toronto, owner of the registered trademark CRUSH
Participaction, p. 179, PARTICIPaction
Pitch and Putt, p. 173, Vancouver Parks Board
Regency Caterers, p. 157, Regency Caterers
Shell, p. 144, Shell Canada Limited
Sweet Cap, p. 113, Imperial Tobacco Limited
Vitalis, p. 141, reprinted by permission of the copyright owner—Bristol-Myers, New York, U.S.A.
Volkswagen, p. 164, Volkswagen of America Inc.

Excerpts from *The Vancouver Sun, The Vancouver Province, Vancouver Magazine, The Georgia Straight, The Globe and Mail, The New York Times, Maclean's, The WestEnder/EastEnder, The Ubyssey, The Buzzer, The Japanese Canadian Citizens Association Bulletin, Jan Morris, Harbour Centre Complex Limited,* and materials from the British Columbia Archives and Records Service are reprinted with permission.